BRUNETTES

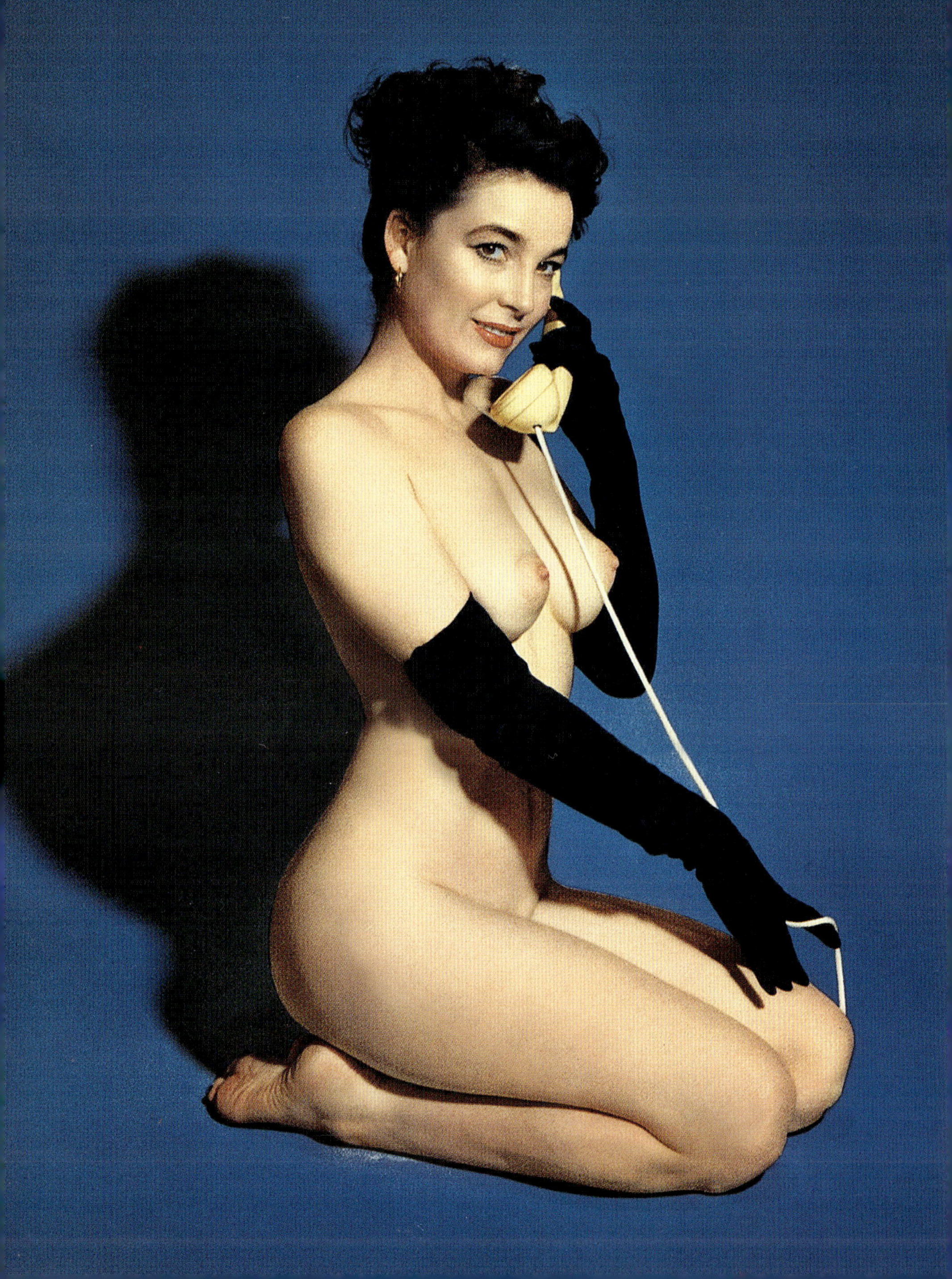

Margie Harrison 1954

PLAYBOY
BRUNETTES

Text by James R. Petersen

CHRONICLE BOOKS
SAN FRANCISCO

LIBRARY OF CONGRESS CATALOGING-IN-PUBLICATION DATA AVAILABLE.
ISBN 0-8118-4857-4

Manufactured in Hong Kong

DISTRIBUTED IN CANADA BY
RAINCOAST BOOKS
9050 SHAUGHNESSY STREET
VANCOUVER, BRITISH COLUMBIA V6P 6E5

1 3 5 7 9 10 8 6 4 2

CHRONICLE BOOKS LLC
85 SECOND STREET
SAN FRANCISCO, CALIFORNIA 94105
www.chroniclebooks.com

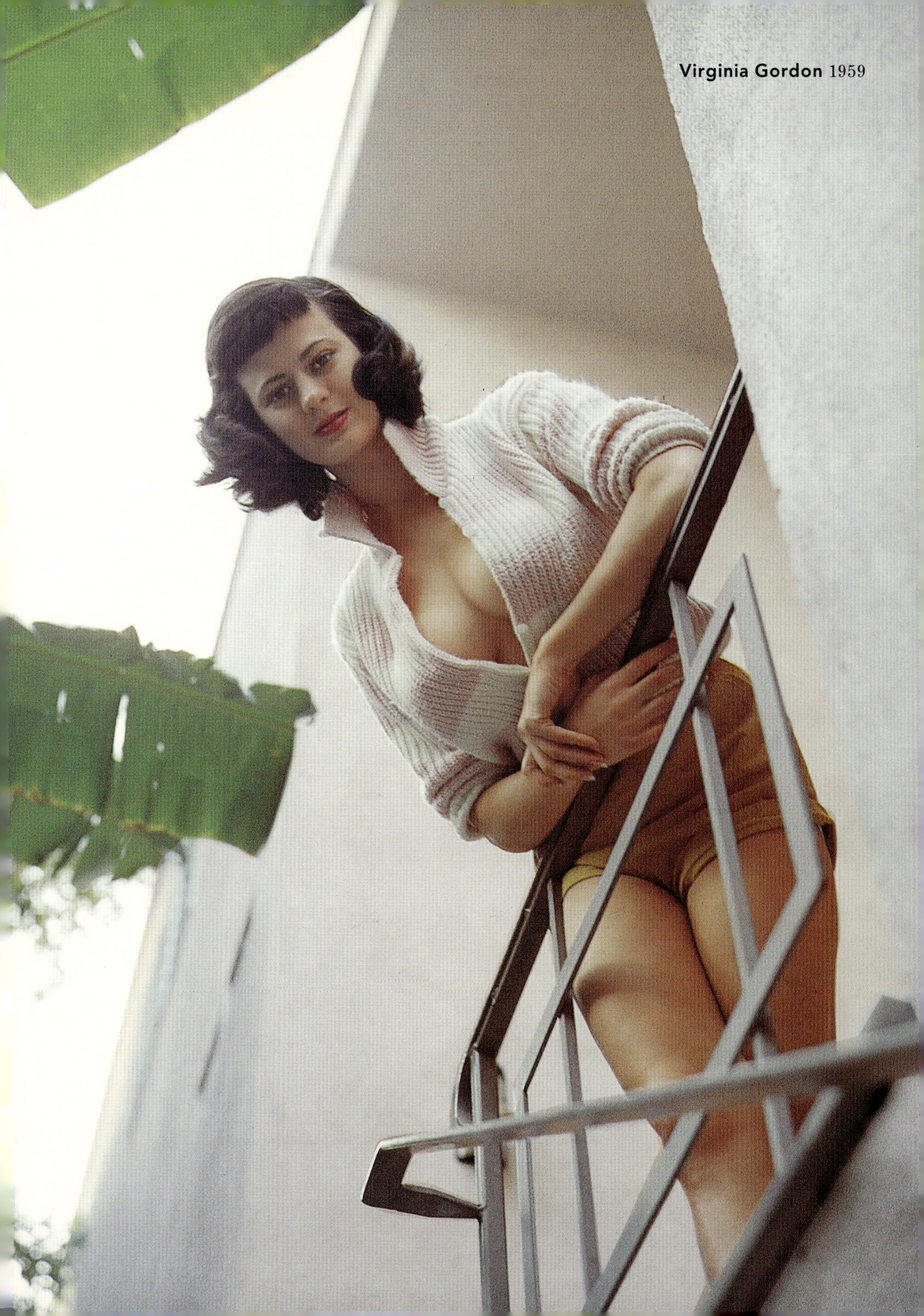

Virginia Gordon 1959

The Mona Lisa is a brunette. What she knows, every brunette knows. And not one has given it away.

If blonde hair is a permission to dream, brunette is a warning. Perhaps it is a simple matter of color. The eye stops at blonde hair, is led away from other, more revealing details. Dark hair frames the face, draws attention to the eyes, the intelligence behind the entertainment. Like the Mona Lisa's, a brunette's eyes follow you around the room. They demand engagement.

Perhaps the power of brunette hair comes from something deeper, more ancient. Consider this entry from an Internet dream dictionary: "Dreaming that you are a brunette indicates that you need to be more down to earth. It may also be symbolic of your sultriness and smoldering sexuality." Do people dream about hair color? No matter. Brunettes live the dream.

Weird science: Scientists claim that the first humans had dark, wavy hair. Red and blonde are more recent evolutions. If God exists and we were created in God's image, She is a brunette.

Brunettes are, in other words, serious business. If not God, then other positions are open. A survey by Clairol found that 75 percent of Americans believe that the first woman president will be a brunette. They are the "face of advice" (think Ann Landers and Dear Abby), have better family lives, and, wouldn't you know it, are more likely to yield at a three-way stop sign. We have no idea what that means, but brunettes, of course, do. Serious? Rosie the Riveter is a brunette.

Quite frankly, we have never understood the stereotype that depicts blondes as sexual bombshells and brunettes as somehow domestic, stable, or, God forbid, boring. If our culture associates blondes with sexual abandon or recklessness, then brunettes represent premeditated, knowledgeable sex, sex with intent. Proof? The original sex goddess, Theda Bara, was a dark-haired vamp who devoured men's souls. Claudette Colbert floated naked in a bath of milk in a sin-and-salvation epic called *The Sign of the Cross.* The controversial hit outraged the Legion of Decency, which called for enforcement of the fledgling Production Code. The result: years of silly, nonbrunette films. Indeed, for all the attention given to the blonde, it was the brunette who caused the most consternation, perhaps because she acted against type, with a vengeance. When Howard Hughes discovered Jane Russell and featured her in *The Outlaw*, would-be censors went ballistic. A judge commented that her breasts floated on the screen like thunderclouds.

In 1933, an Austrian actress named Hedwig Kiesler was caught in the throes of *Ecstasy*, her face surrounded by glorious dark hair. She allowed the camera to capture what was the first on-screen climax, a moment not repeated for decades. The Treasury Department seized the film, calling it a glorification of sexual intercourse. We'd call it a glorification of brunette. The actress changed her name to Hedy Lamarr and continued to beguile audiences.

Moviegoers had no shortage of American brunettes to revere. Natalie Wood's tresses were the splendor in *Splendor in the Grass*. Although historians say that the Queen of the Nile was a blonde (who dyed her locks with henna), Elizabeth Taylor portrayed a raven-haired Cleopatra. She wrecked a marriage or six. In *Boy on a Dolphin*, Sophia Loren emerged from the sea in a water-soaked dress that defined the sensuous. Brunettes had a way of doing the unexpected: Barbara Carrera taking off her blouse in *I, the Jury*, Phoebe Cates diving into the pool in *Fast Times at Ridgmont High*, Jennifer Beals' trick with her clothes in *Flashdance*. Maria Schneider rewrote the rules for cinematic sex (and what mainstream movies would allow) in *Last Tango in Paris*. Brunettes have killer moves and give nothing to the competition. They have a way of branding the eyes of an entire generation.

Before we settle on a consensus stereotype, remember that brunette is not a single color. Brunettes play with a palette that includes names like Amazon Indigo, Nutmeg, and Spiced Shadow. The shade ranges from light—Tawny Bronze, Amber Shimmer—to dark—Pepper, Rich Sable, Sapphire. Go back to the one about Amazon Indigo. Ancient myths and more recent pop culture creations suggest the power of brunette. Wonder Woman. Xena, warrior princess. Lara Croft. Trinity of *The Matrix.* Long before she became a spokeswoman for cell phones, Catherine Zeta-Jones clashed swords with Antonio Banderas in *The Mask of Zorro*. The bottom line: Brunettes look better with weapons. Brunettes do not need to be rescued. They obey the primal rule, the one that says, "The only requirement is keeping up."

Forget forever the notion that gentlemen prefer blondes. One study found that dark-haired men prefer brunettes, while blond-haired men fall for both blondes and brunettes. A few years ago, Sophie Cahill, the reigning Miss Wales and a natural brunette, conducted an unofficial experiment. She walked the streets of her home city first as a brunette, then as a blonde. She received more wolf whistles as a brunette.

In June 2004, Evian water conducted a survey to determine the most beautiful woman of all time. Audrey Hepburn was number one, placed in the top ten by more than 76 percent of the beauty experts who voted. Indeed, 46 percent of the icons placed in the number one spot by panel members were brunette—compared to 32 percent blonde and 22 percent redhead.

You hold in your hands some two decades of brunettes. *Playboy* launched its first issue in the fifties, a decade that made a fetish of blonde. And yet the magazine noticed brunettes from the start: 45.5 percent of the centerfolds have had brown hair, another 2.7 percent classic raven hair—edging out blondes at 44.4 percent. They run the gamut, from sleek to statuesque, knowing to innocent, pert to provocative. Study these pictures. What does their silence tell you? Like the Mona Lisa, these brunettes prefer to let you wonder.

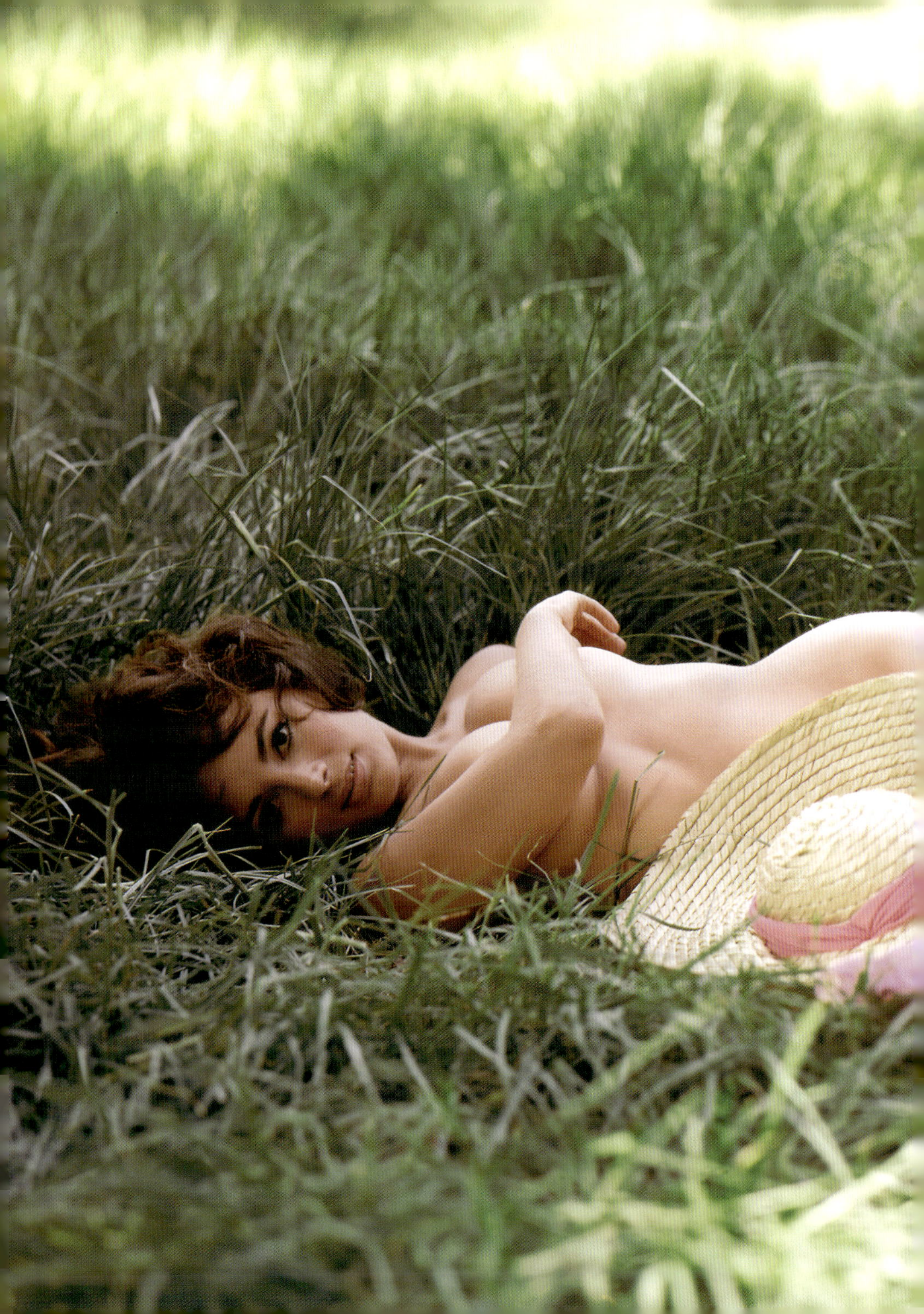

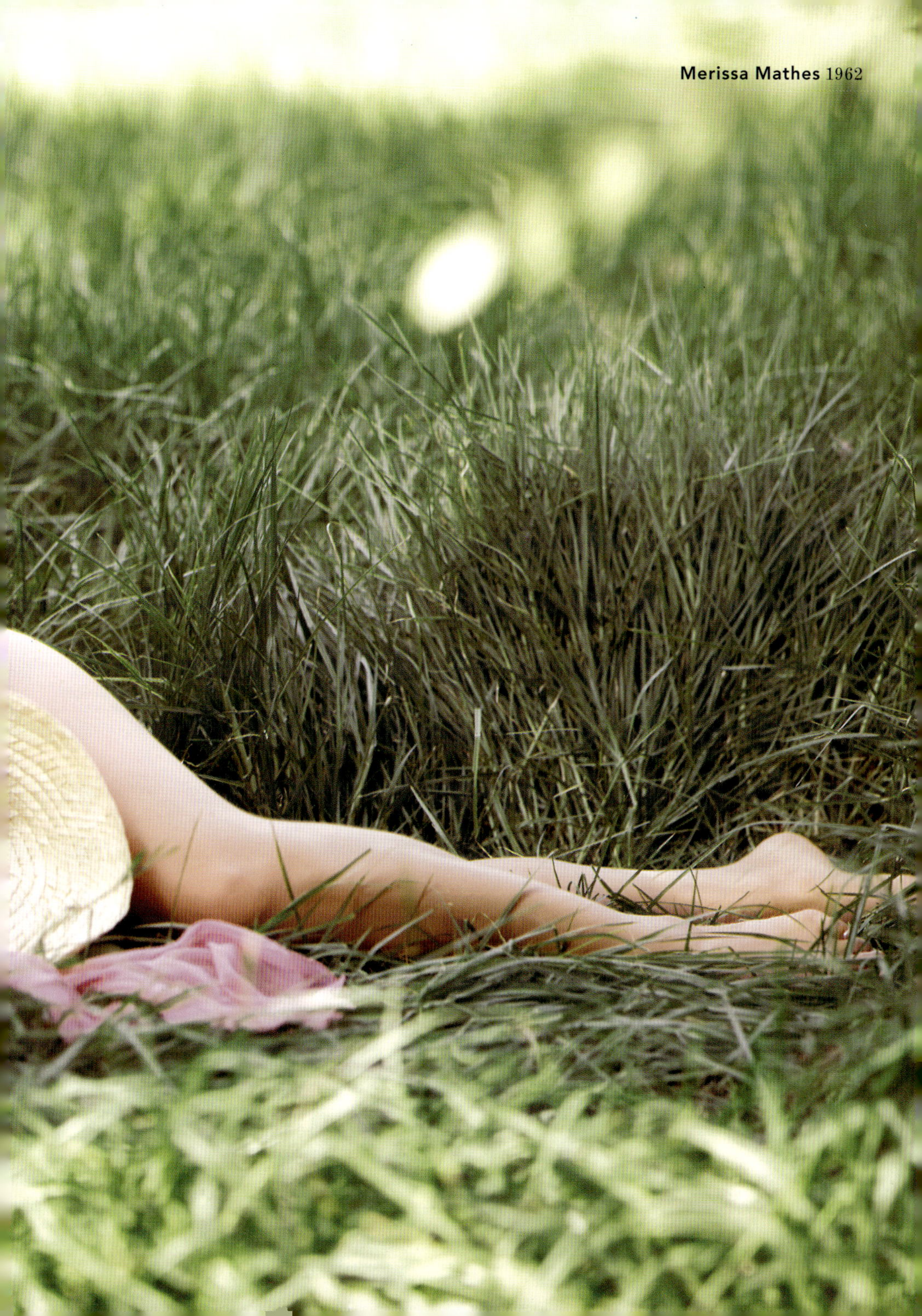

Merissa Mathes 1962

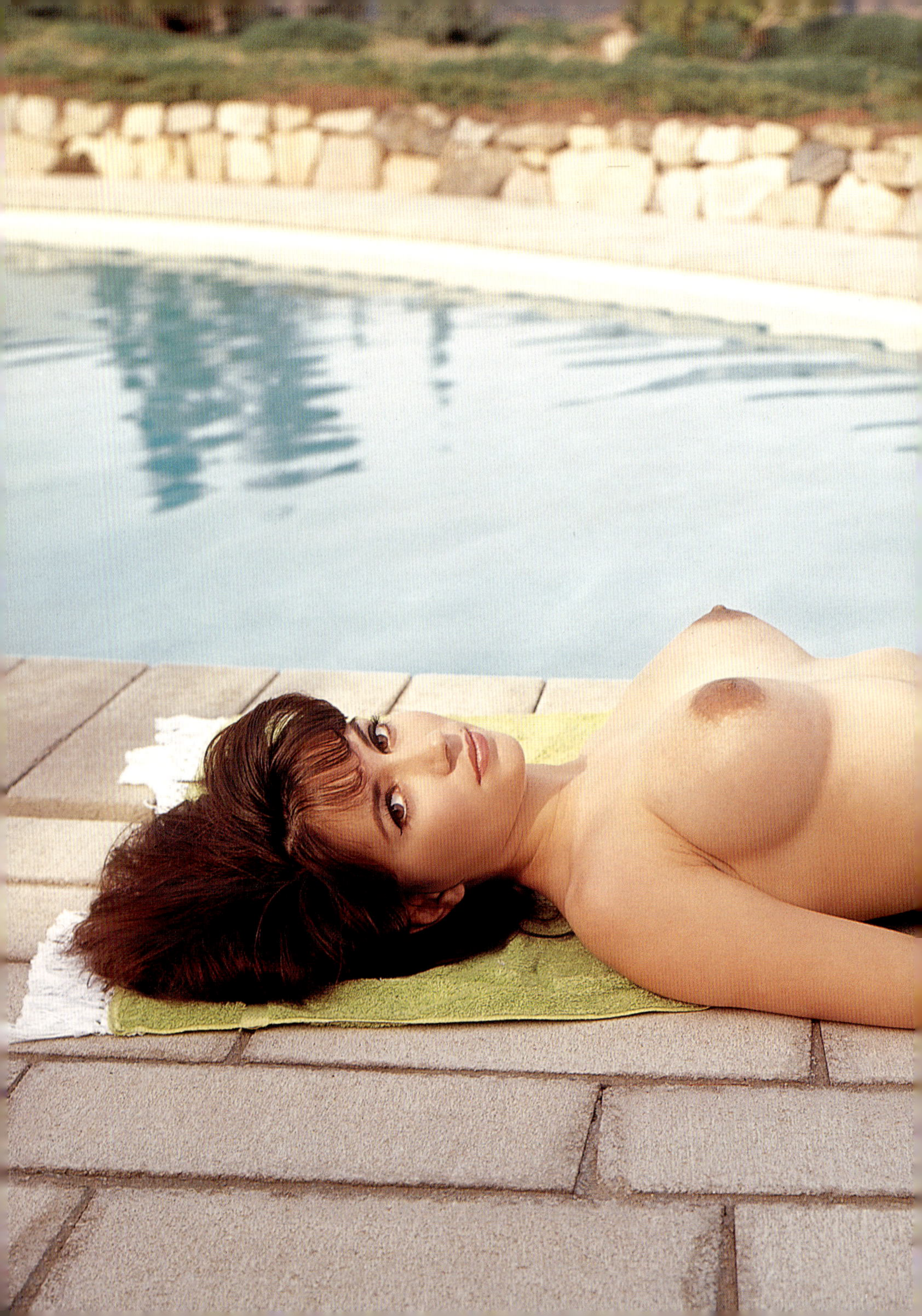

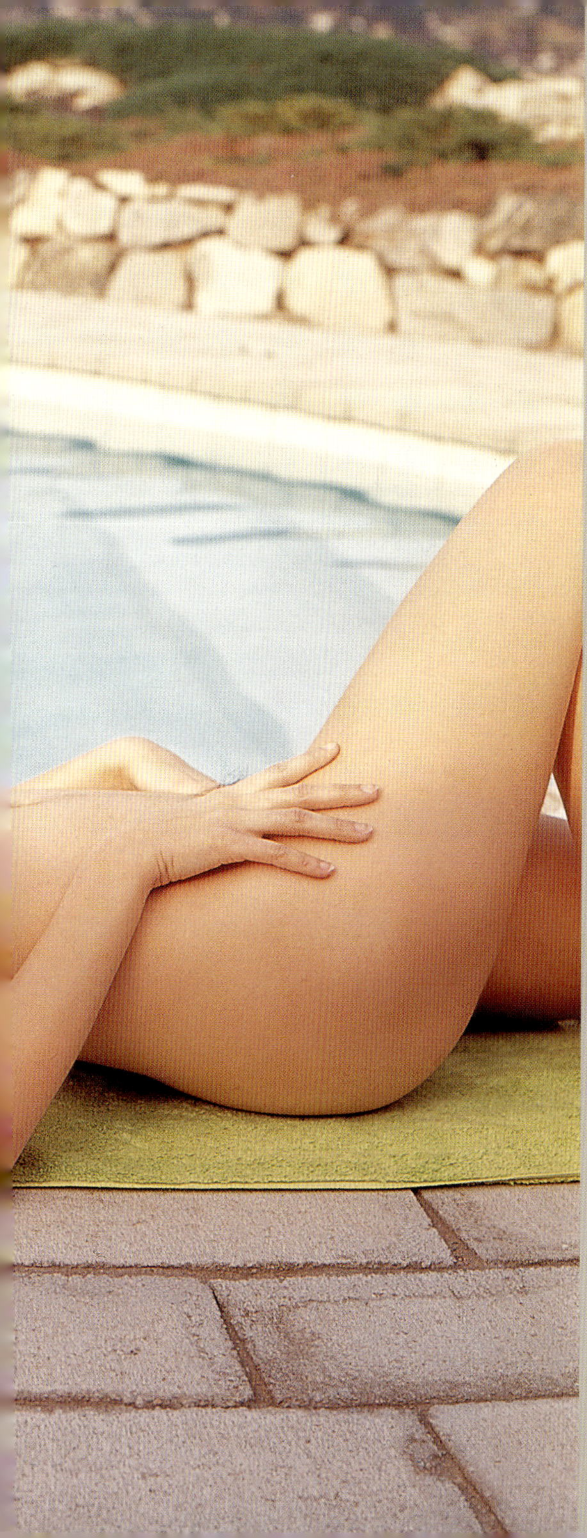

NORA CHARLES:

"You got types?"

NICK CHARLES:

"Only you darling, lanky brunettes with wicked jaws."

WILLIAM POWELL TO MYRNA LOY IN *THE THIN MAN*

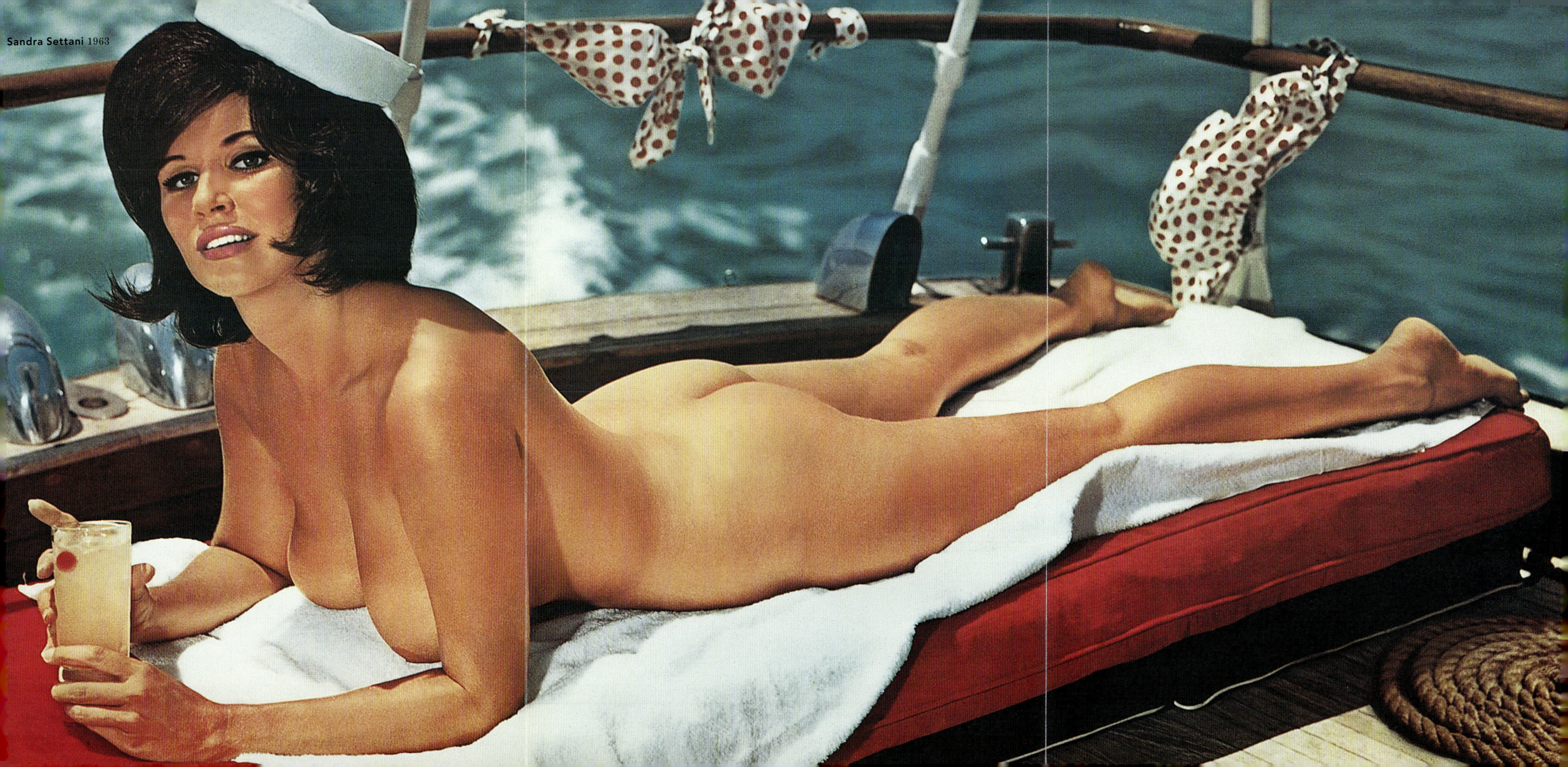

Sandra Settani 1963

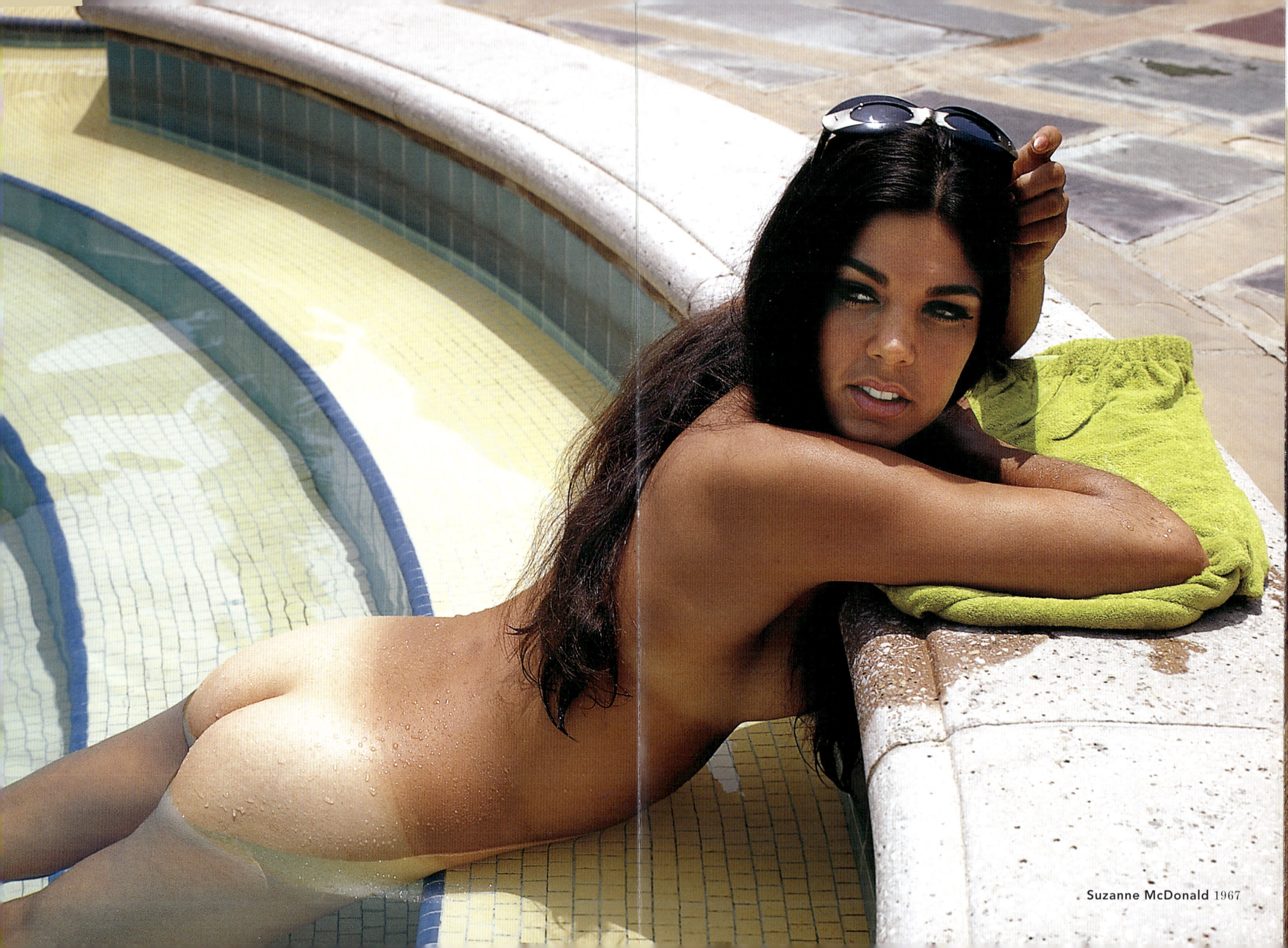

Suzanne McDonald 1967

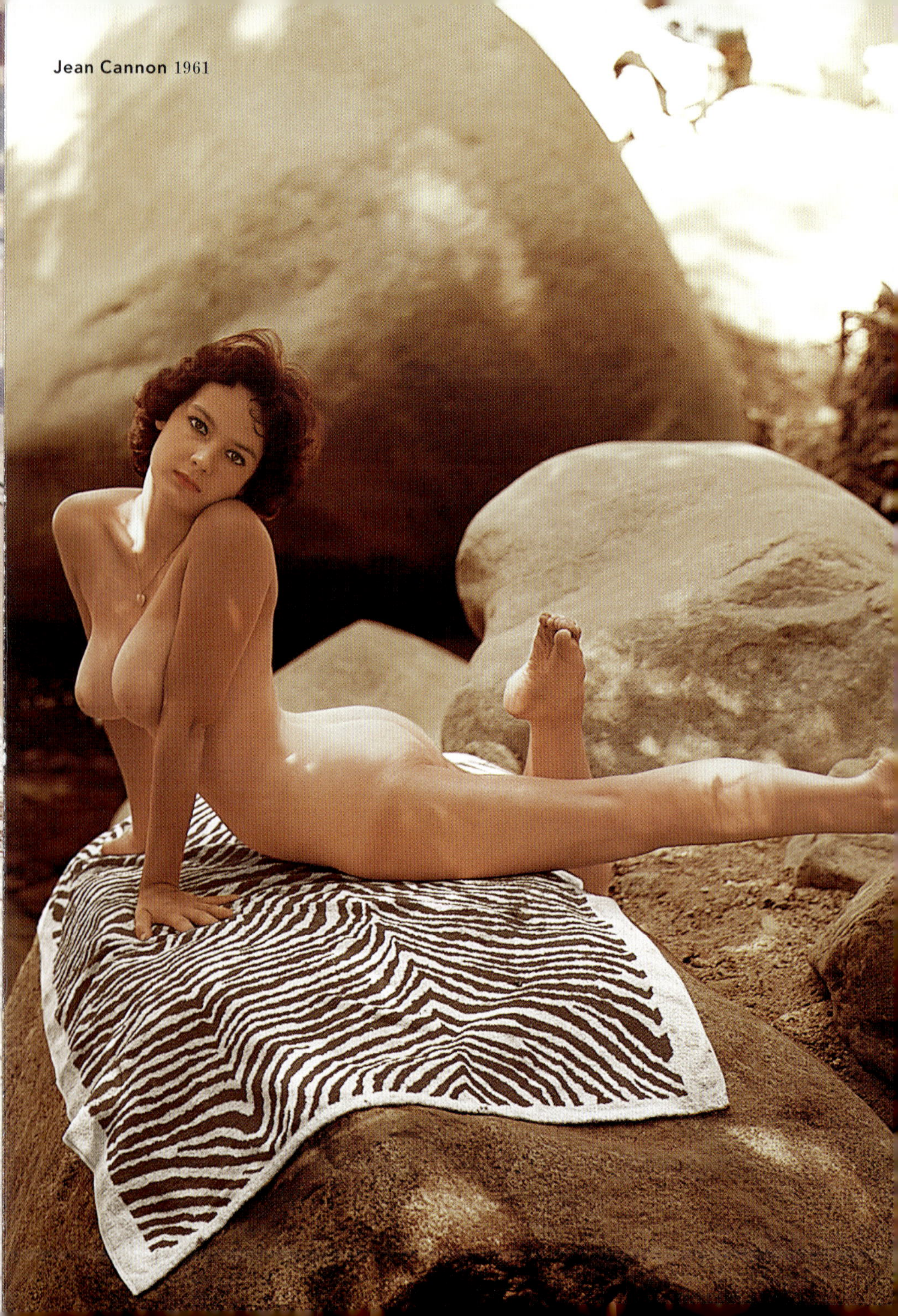

Jean Cannon 1961

"Blown hair is sweet,
brown hair over the mouth blown,
Lilac and brown hair."

T. S. ELIOT

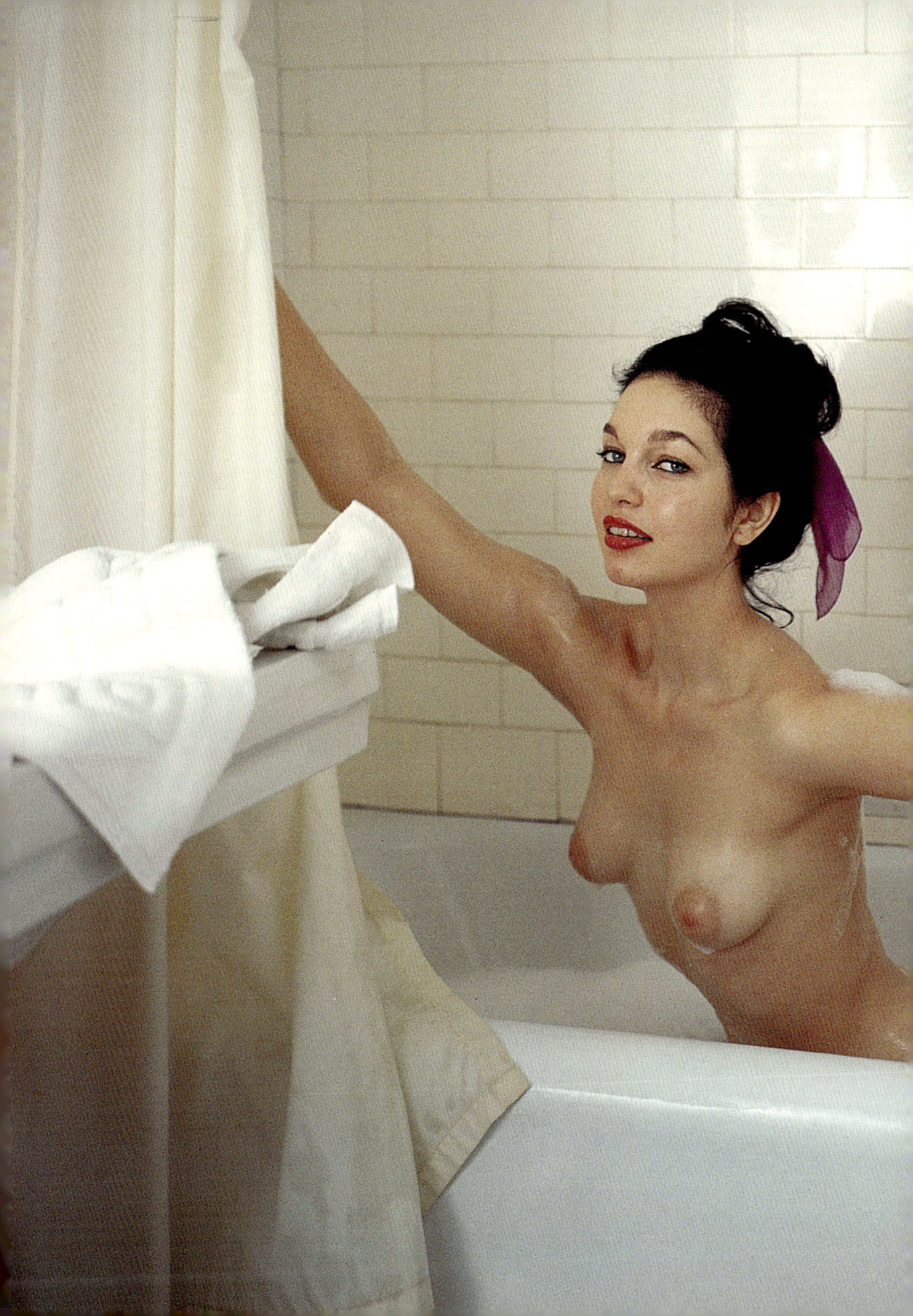

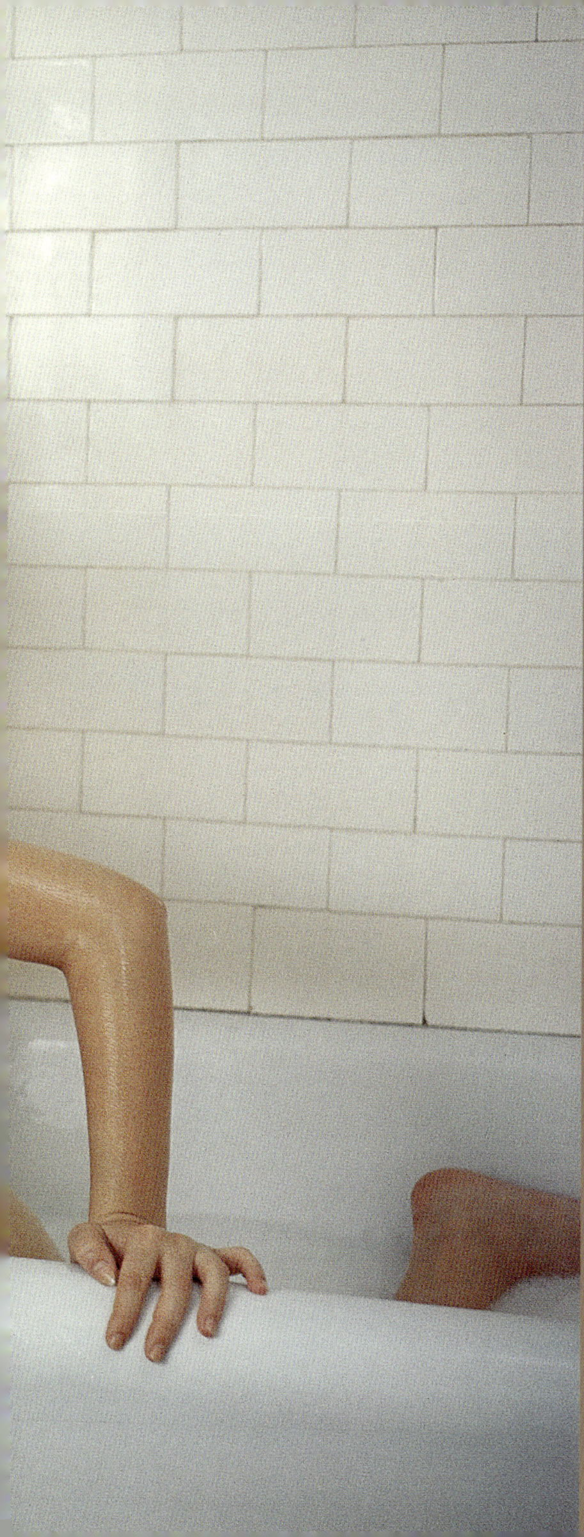

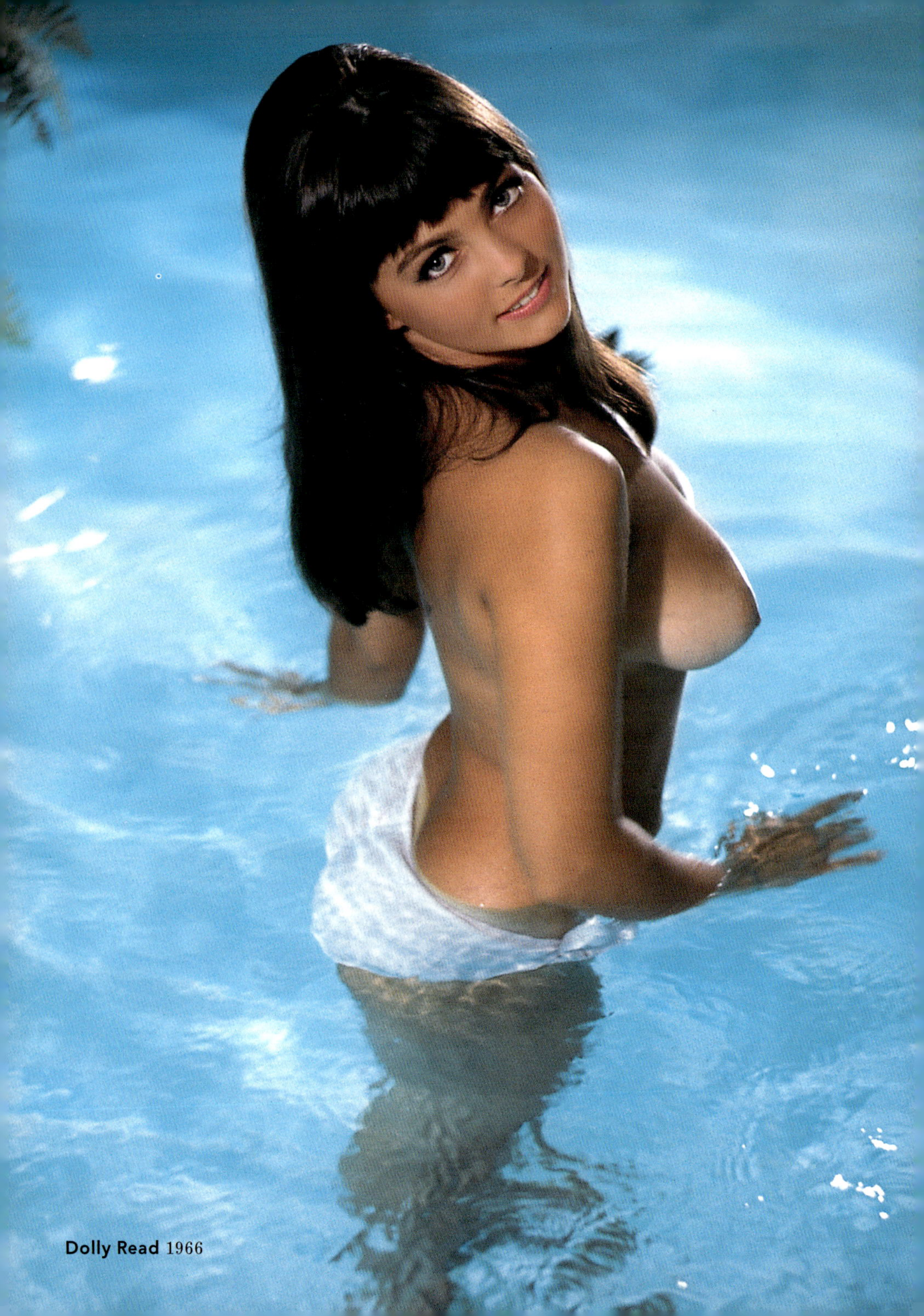
Dolly Read 1966

"Brunettes have the scent of ebony."

AUGUSTIN GALOPIN, *LE PARFUM DE LA FEMME*

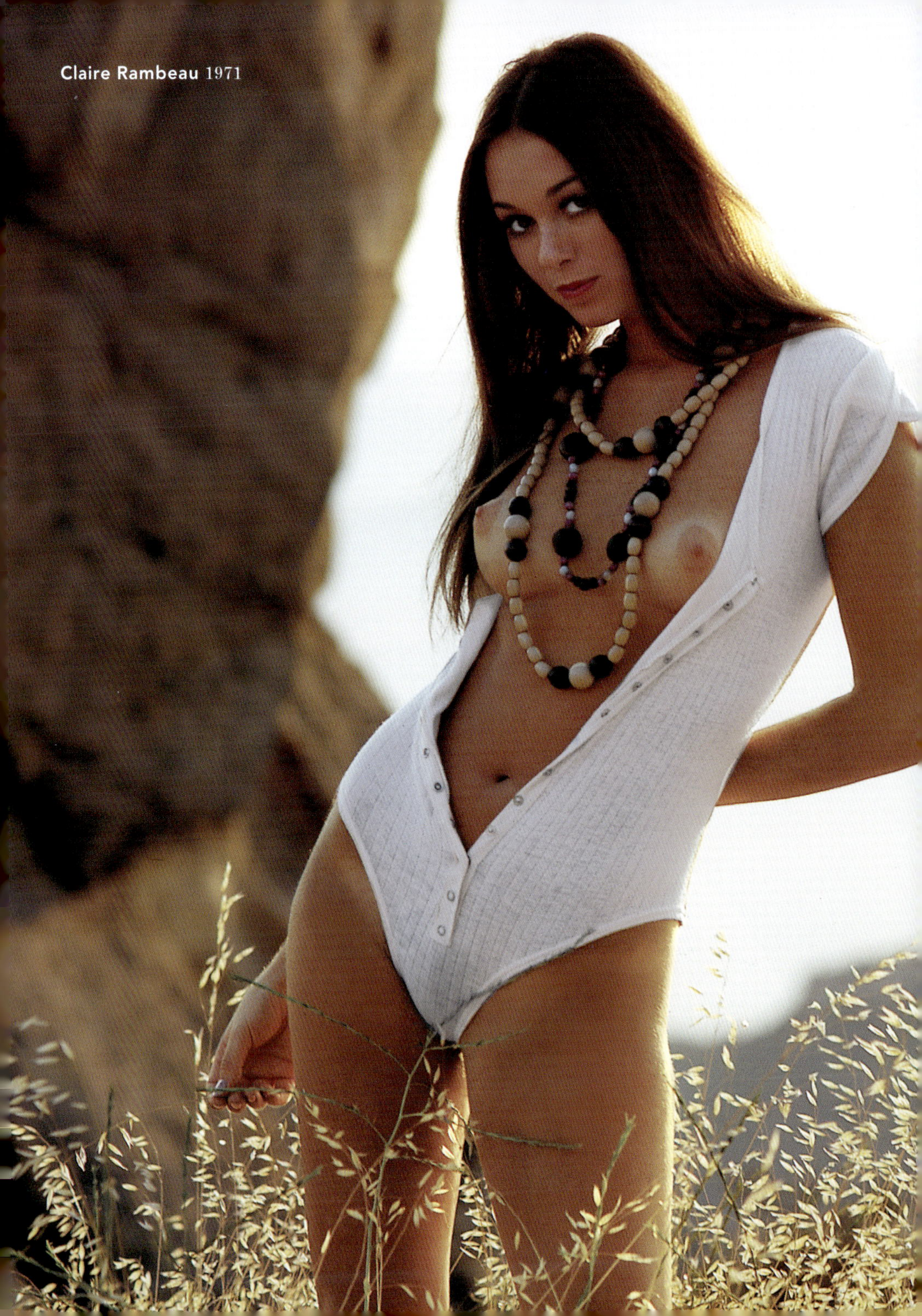

Claire Rambeau 1971

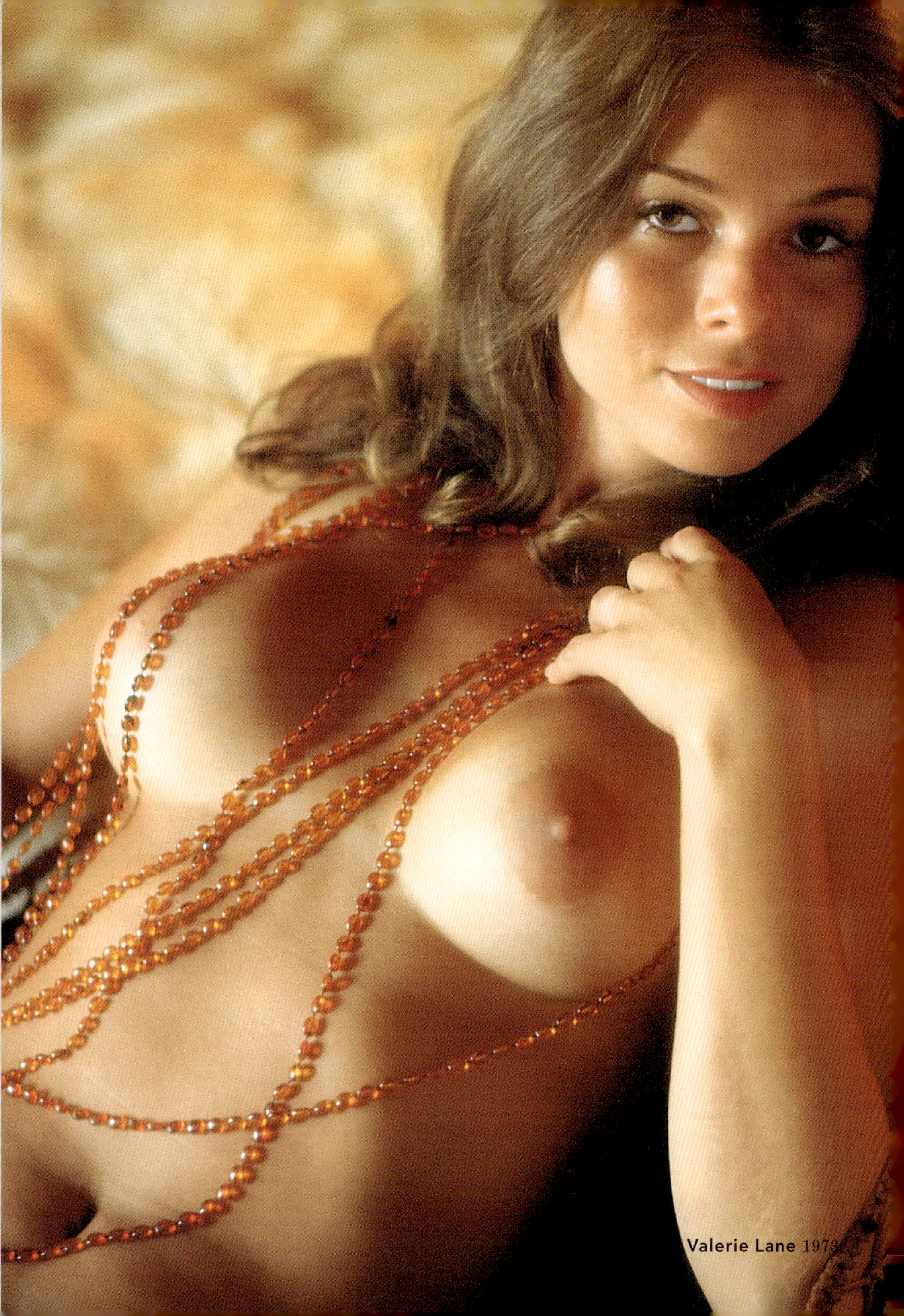

Valerie Lane 1973

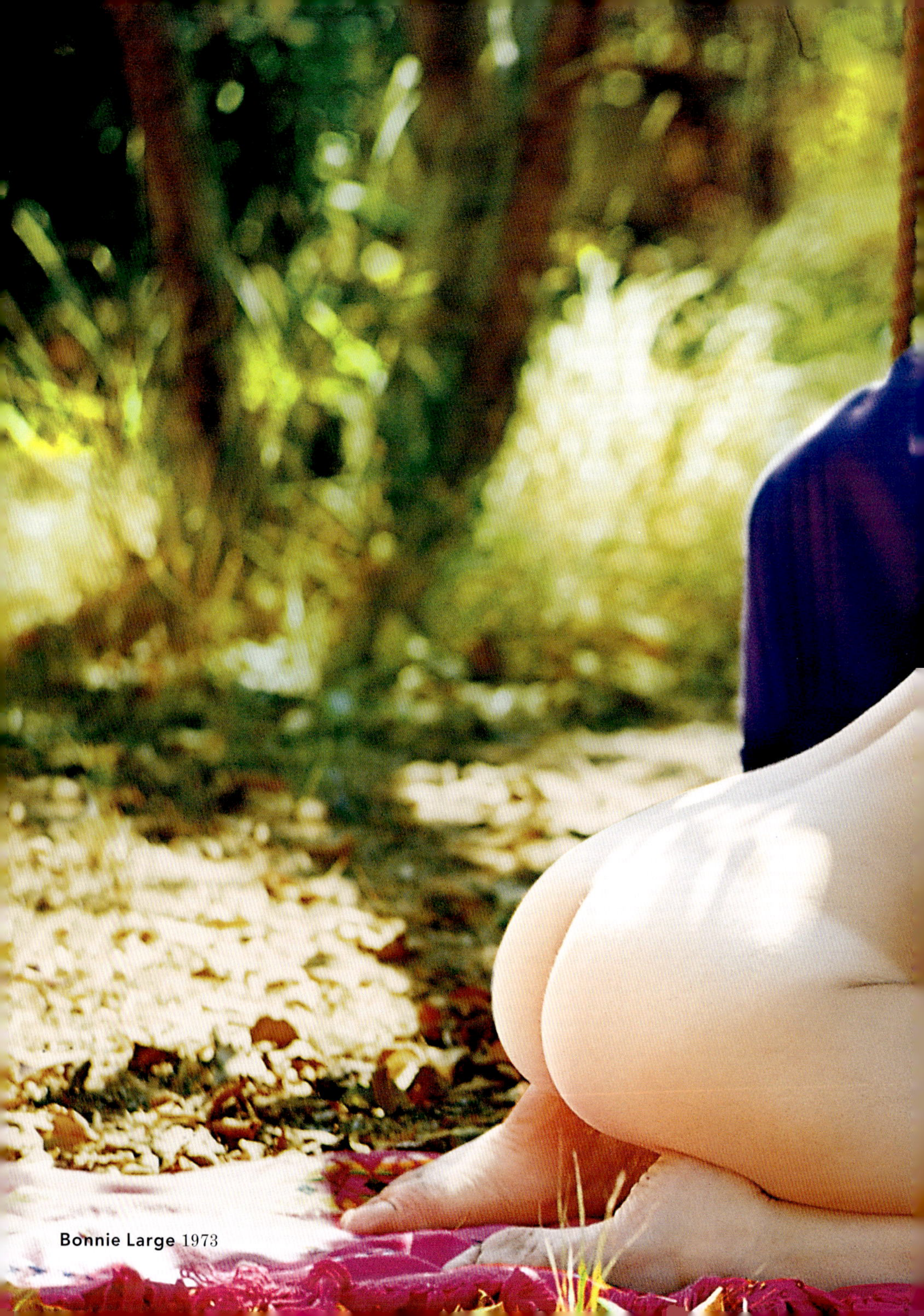

Bonnie Large 1973

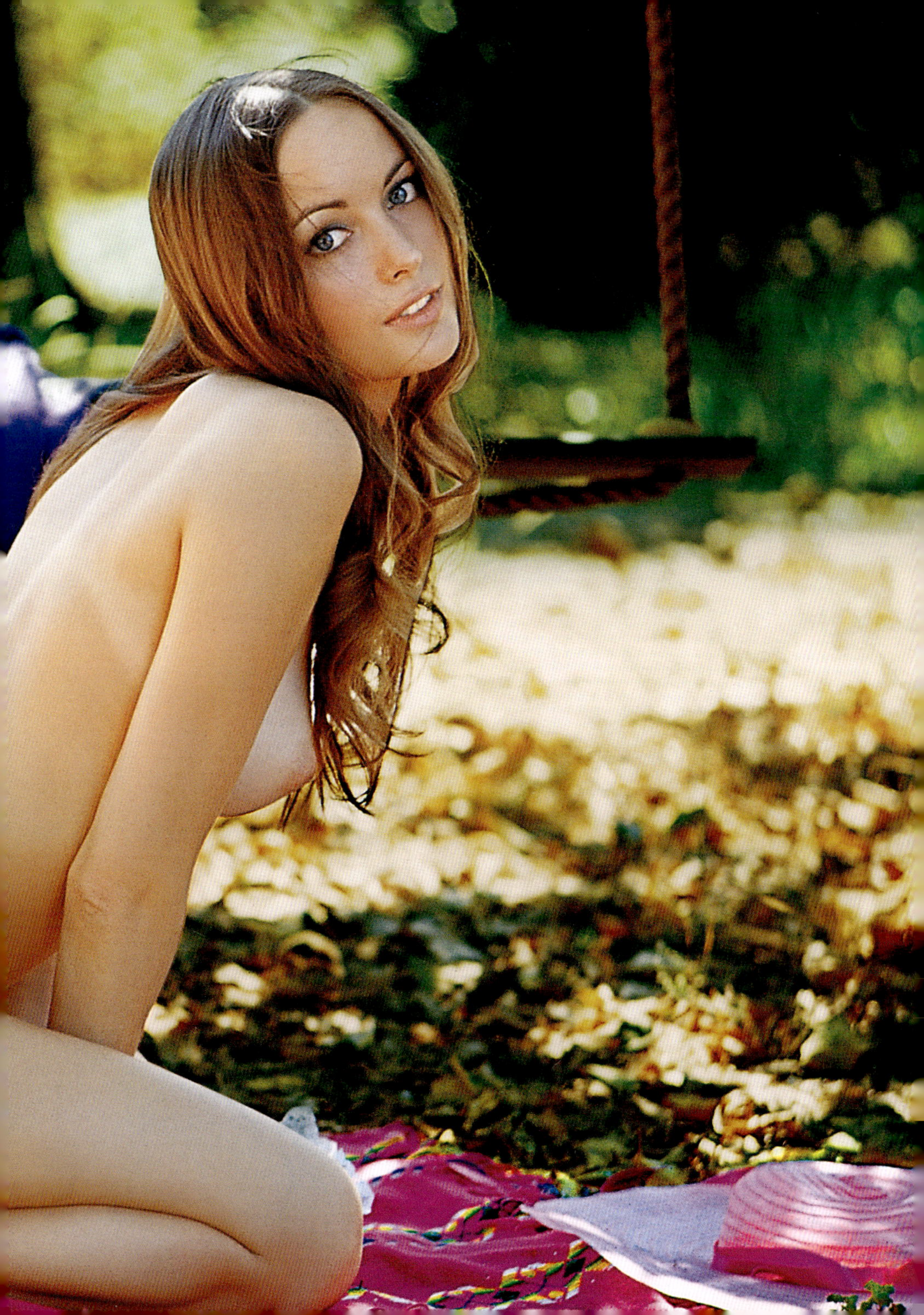

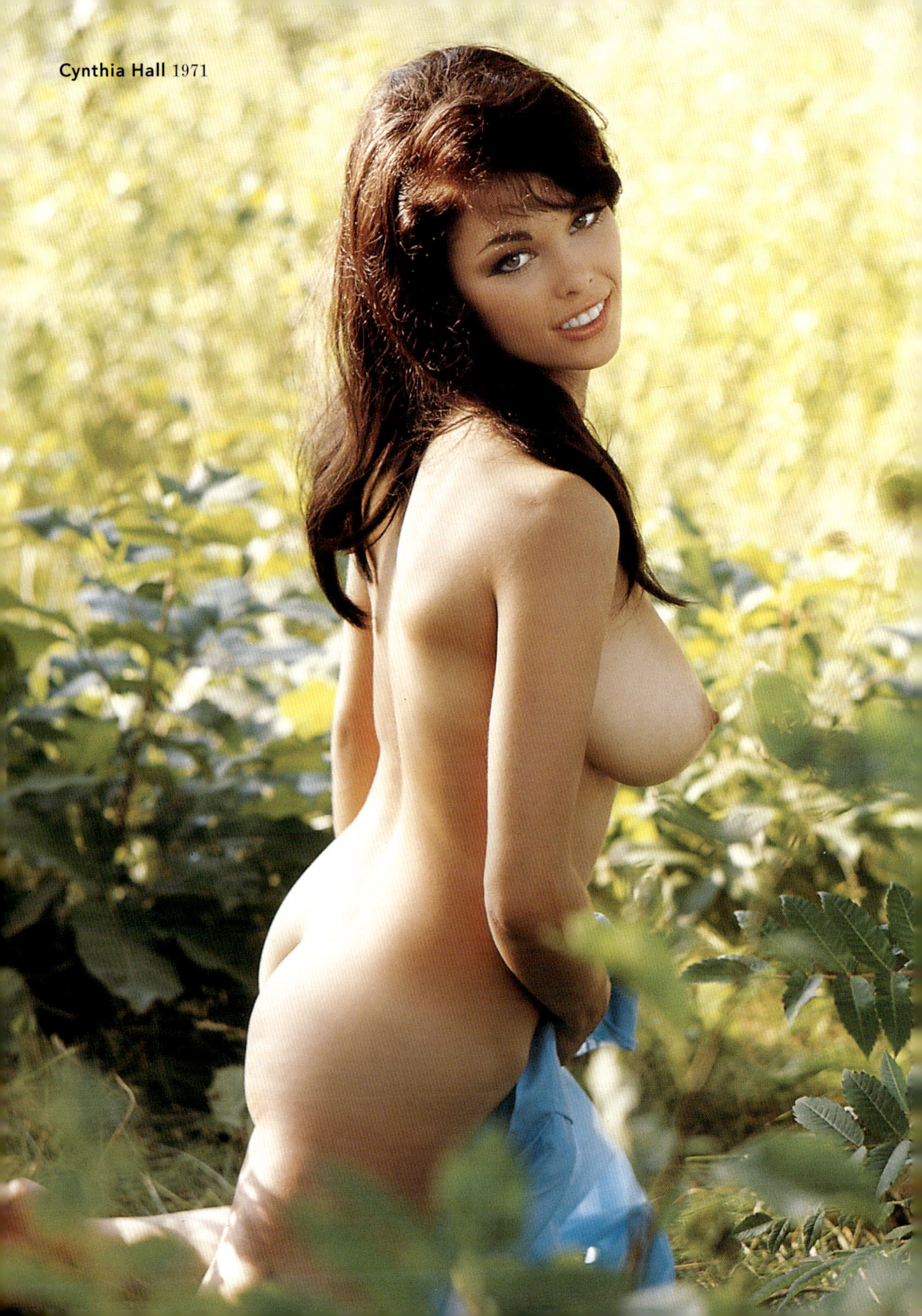

Cynthia Hall 1971

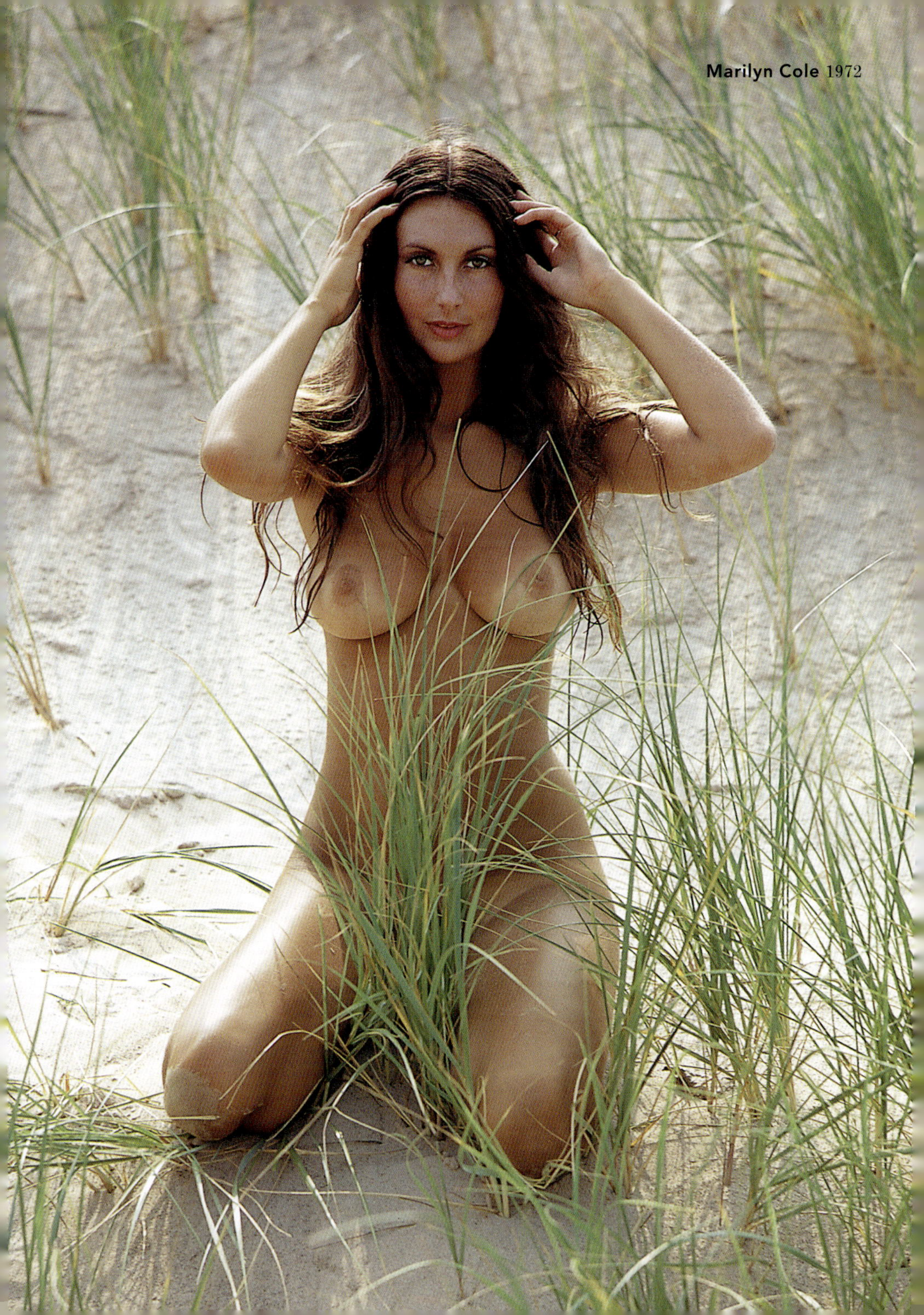

Marilyn Cole 1972

"Oh! my God! the down,
The soft young down of her, the brown,
The brown of her—her eyes, her hair,
her hair . . ."

CHARLOTTE MEW, BRITISH POET

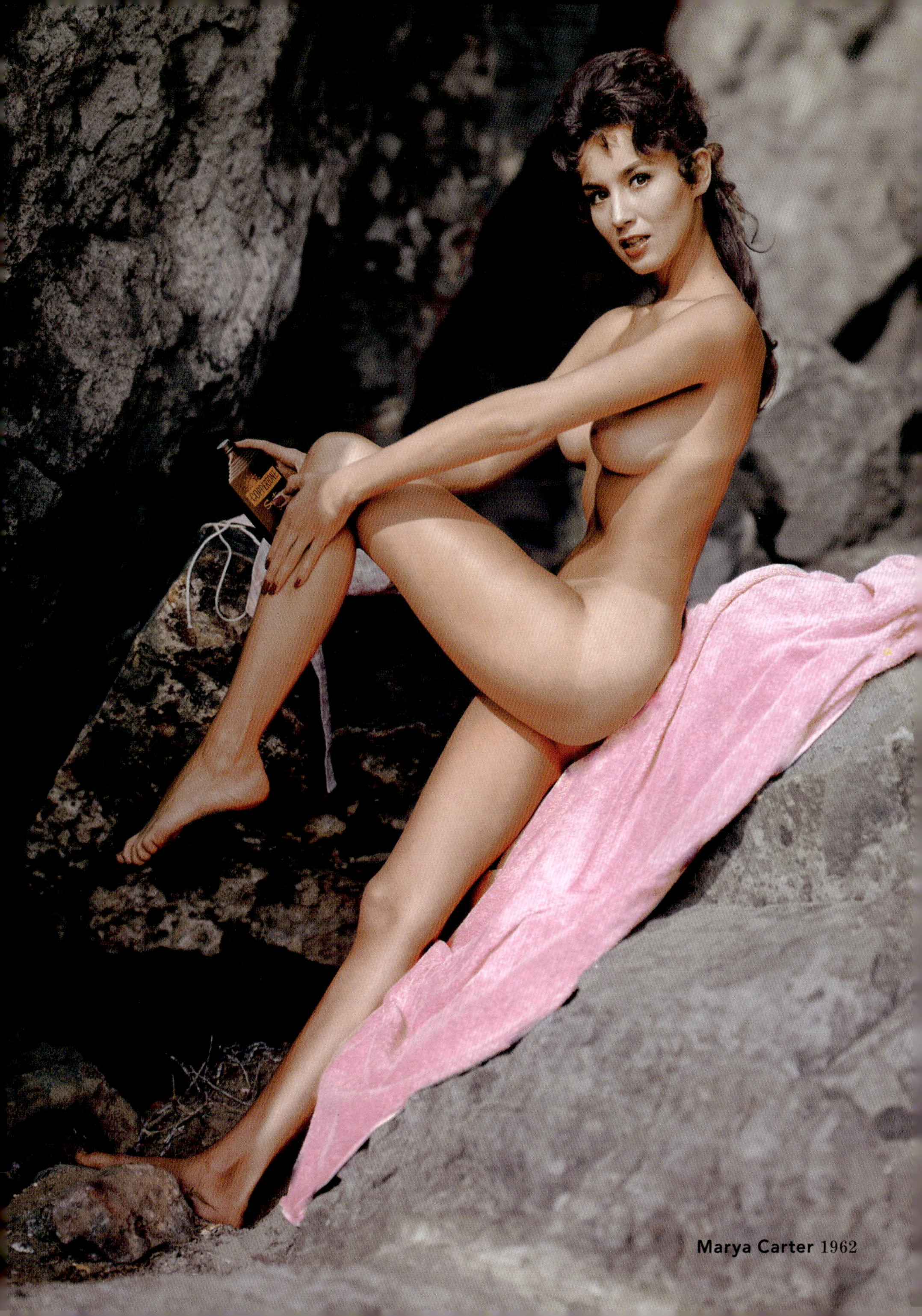

Marya Carter 1962

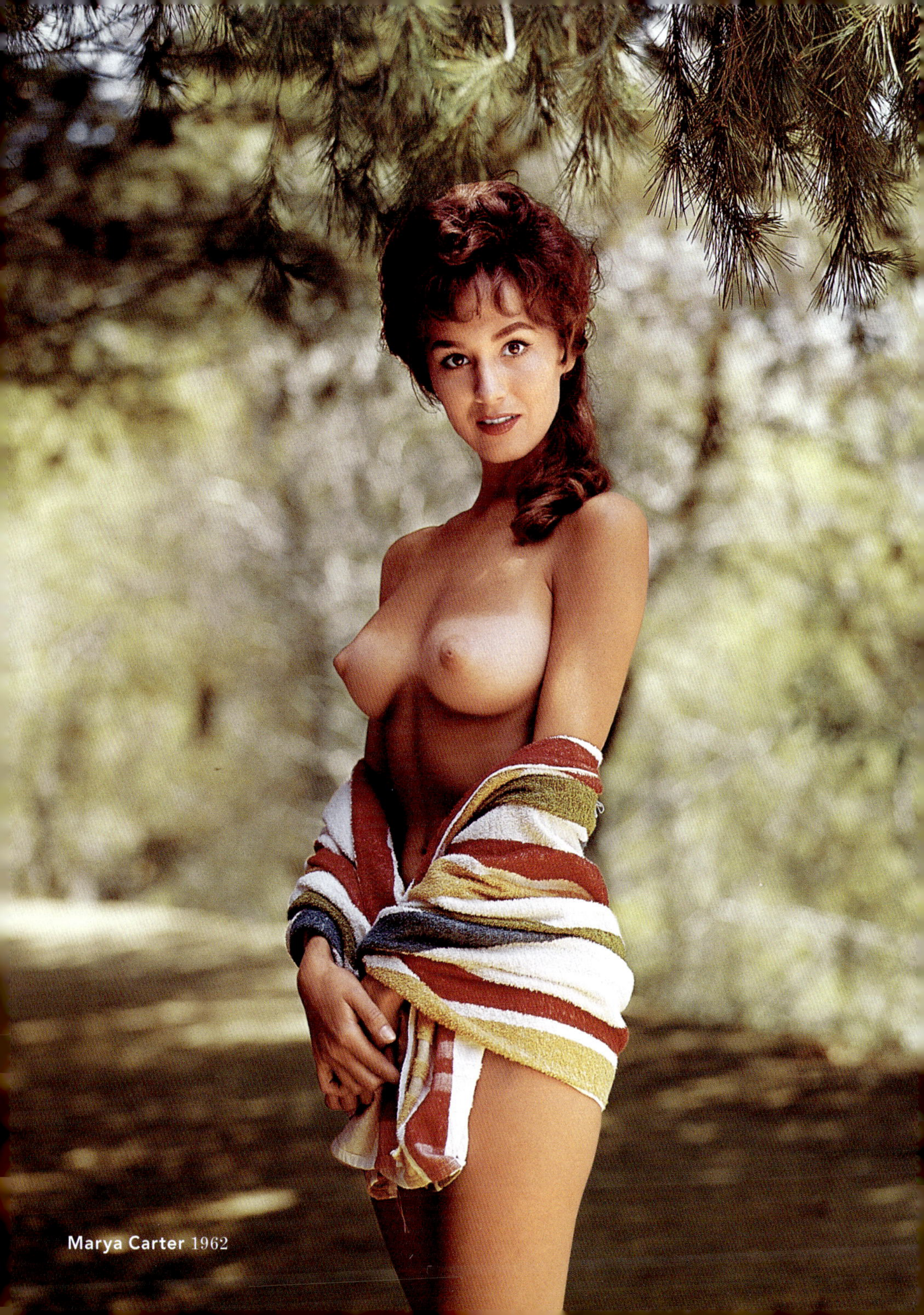

Marya Carter 1962

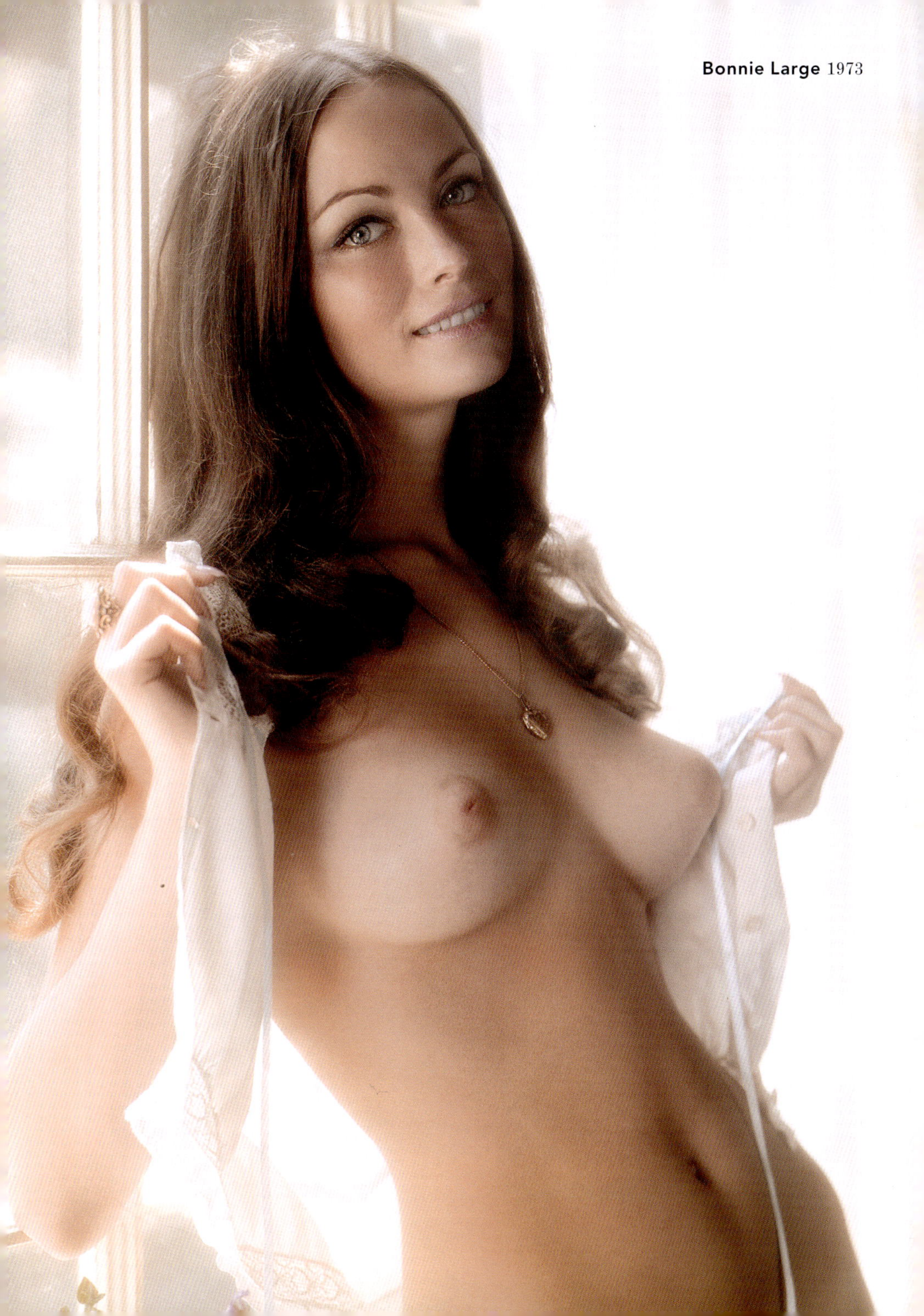

Bonnie Large 1973

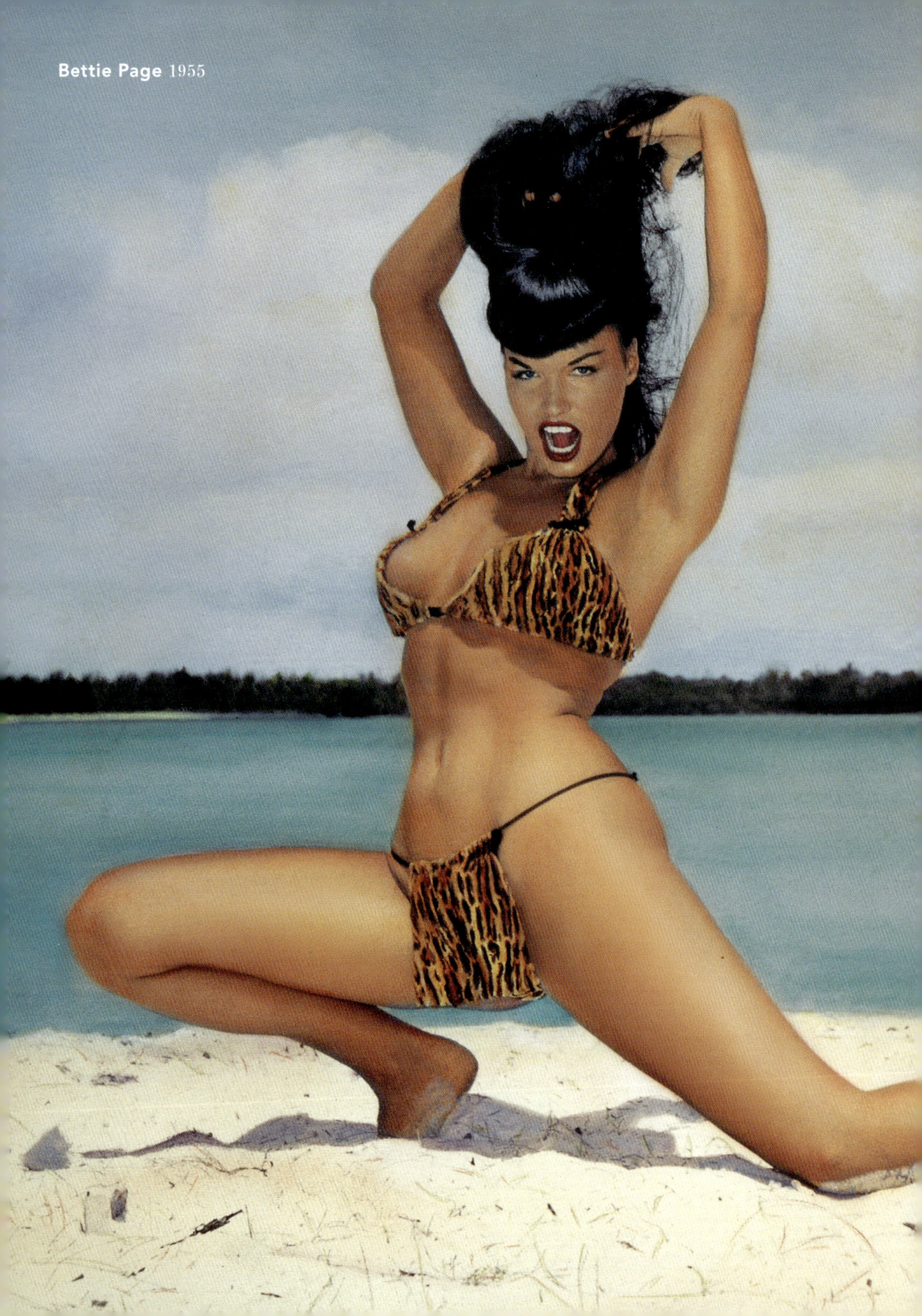
Bettie Page 1955

"Bettie Page was number one. I have never known another model who had better knowledge of her body or how to work with it to make it look so good. Her skin was perfect, no blemishes. Perfect nose, beautiful straight teeth, and gleaming, shiny black hair that was always in place, always."

BUNNY YEAGER, PHOTOGRAPHER

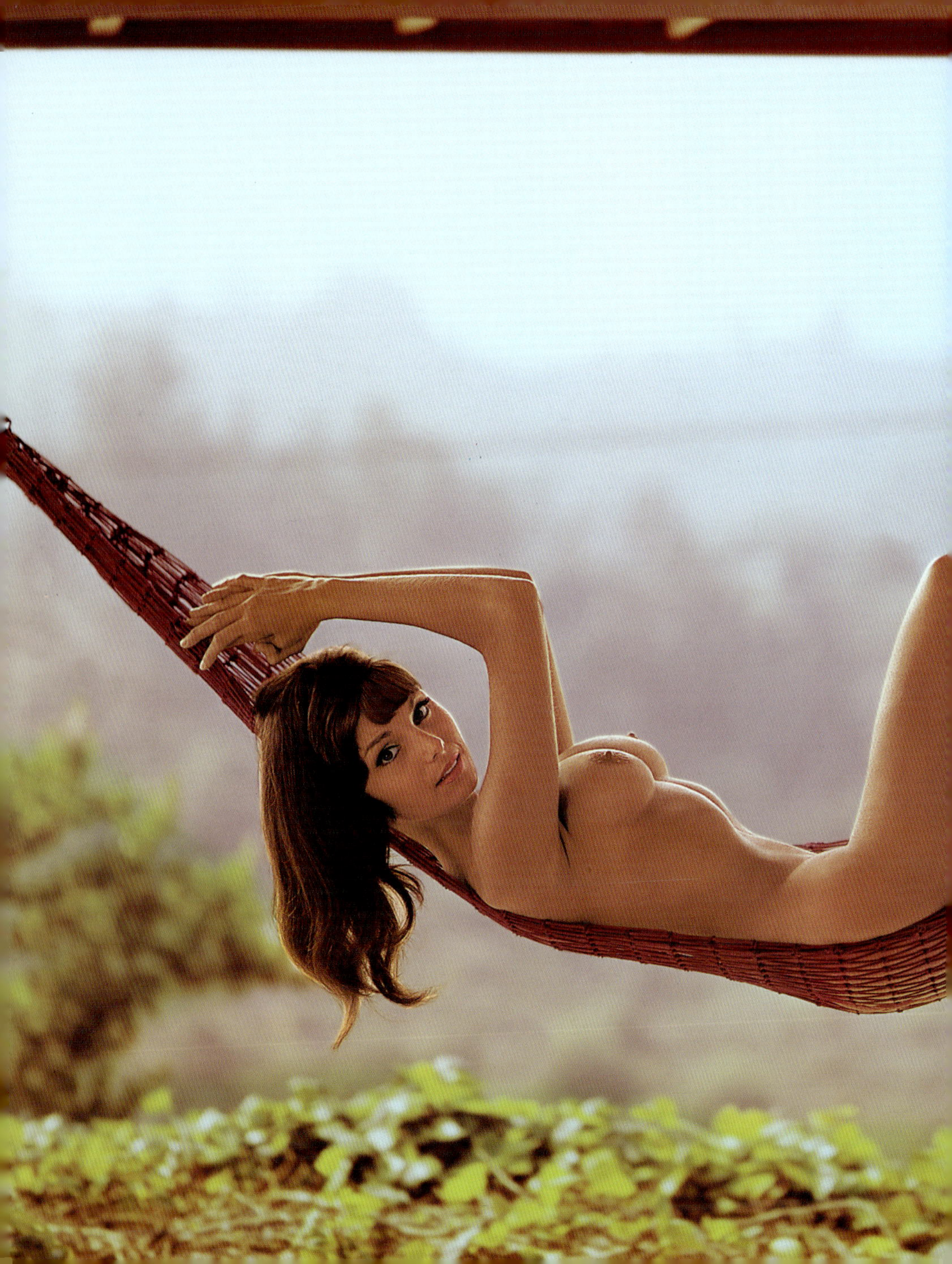

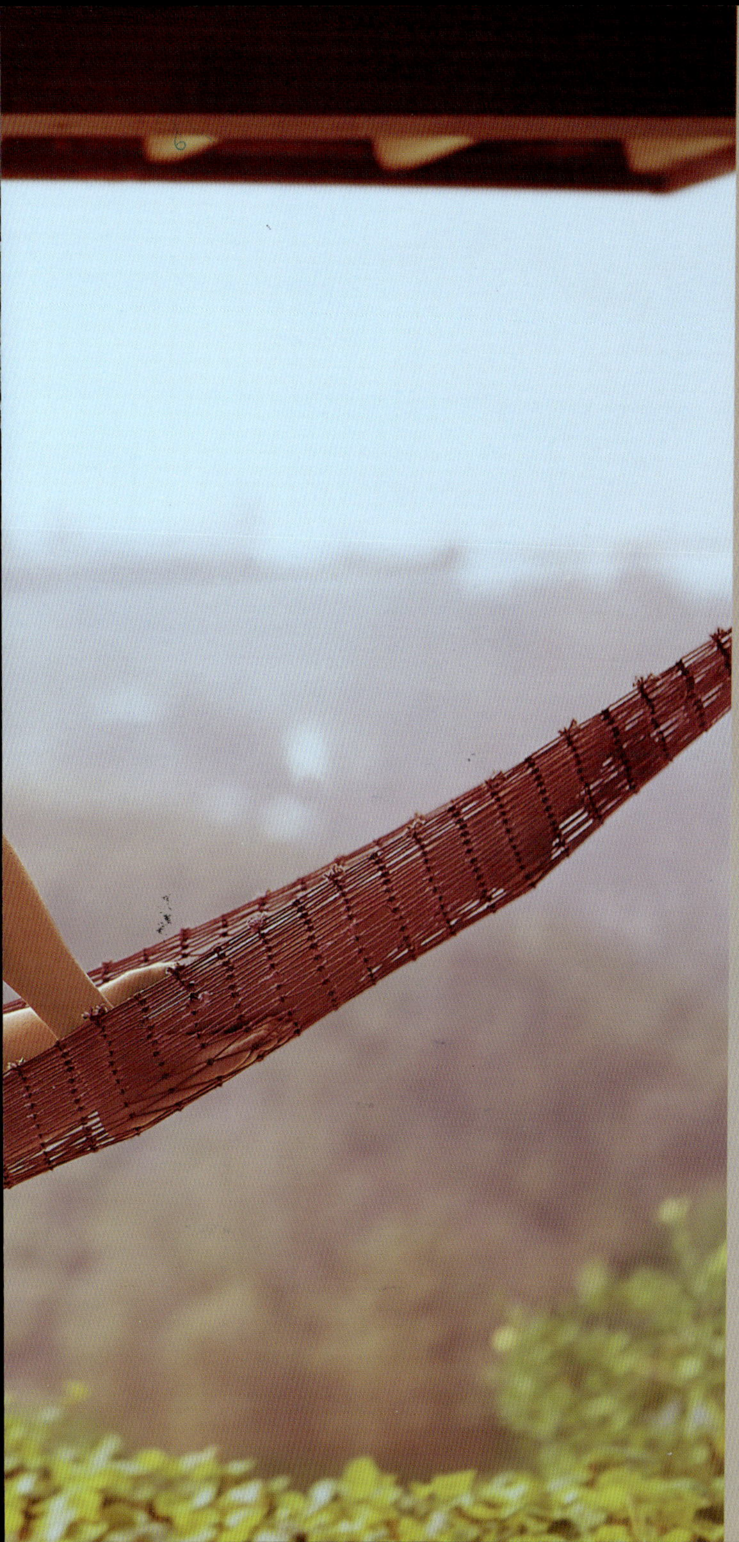

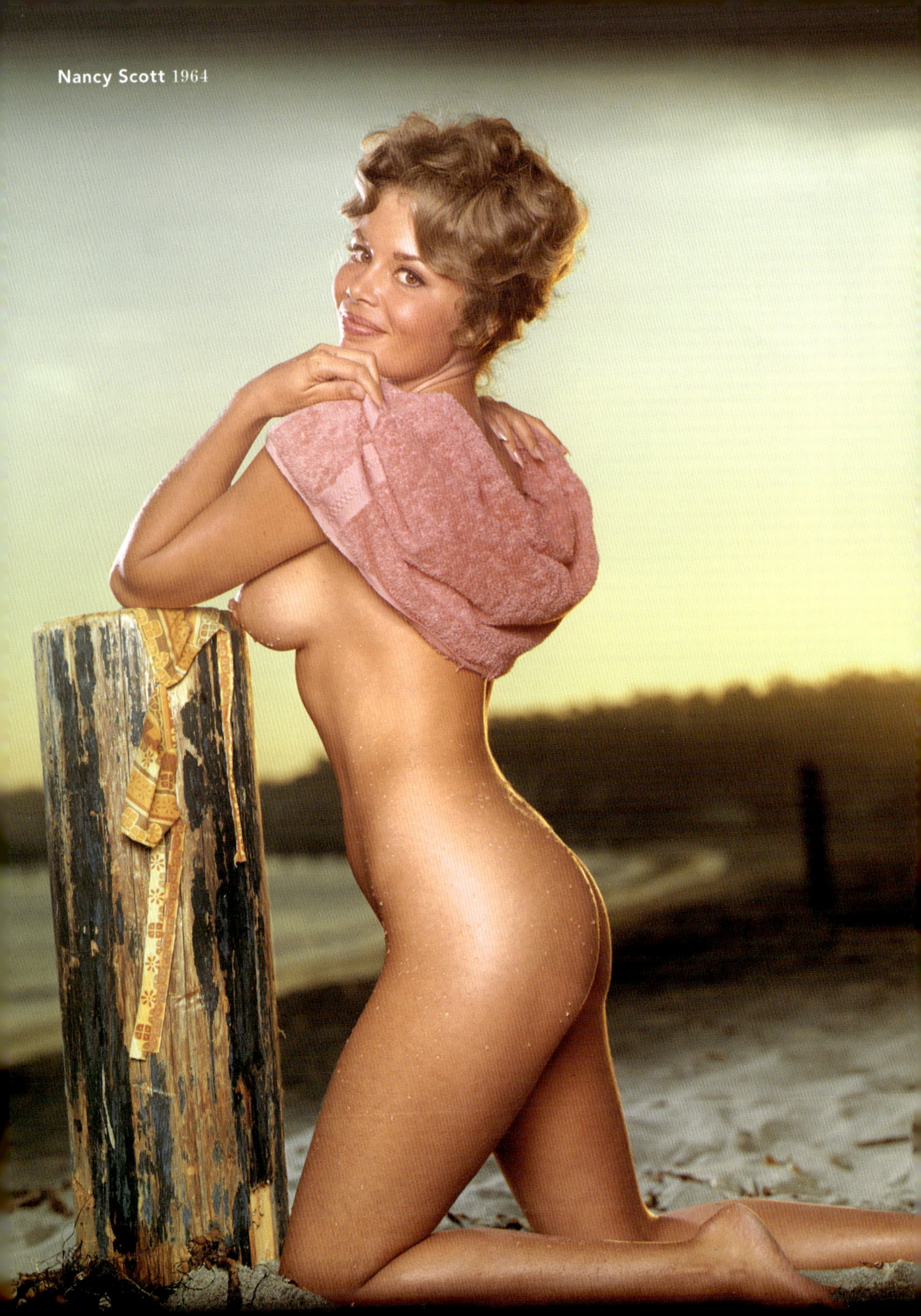

Nancy Scott 1964

"I dream of Jeannie
with the light brown hair."

STEPHEN COLLINS FOSTER

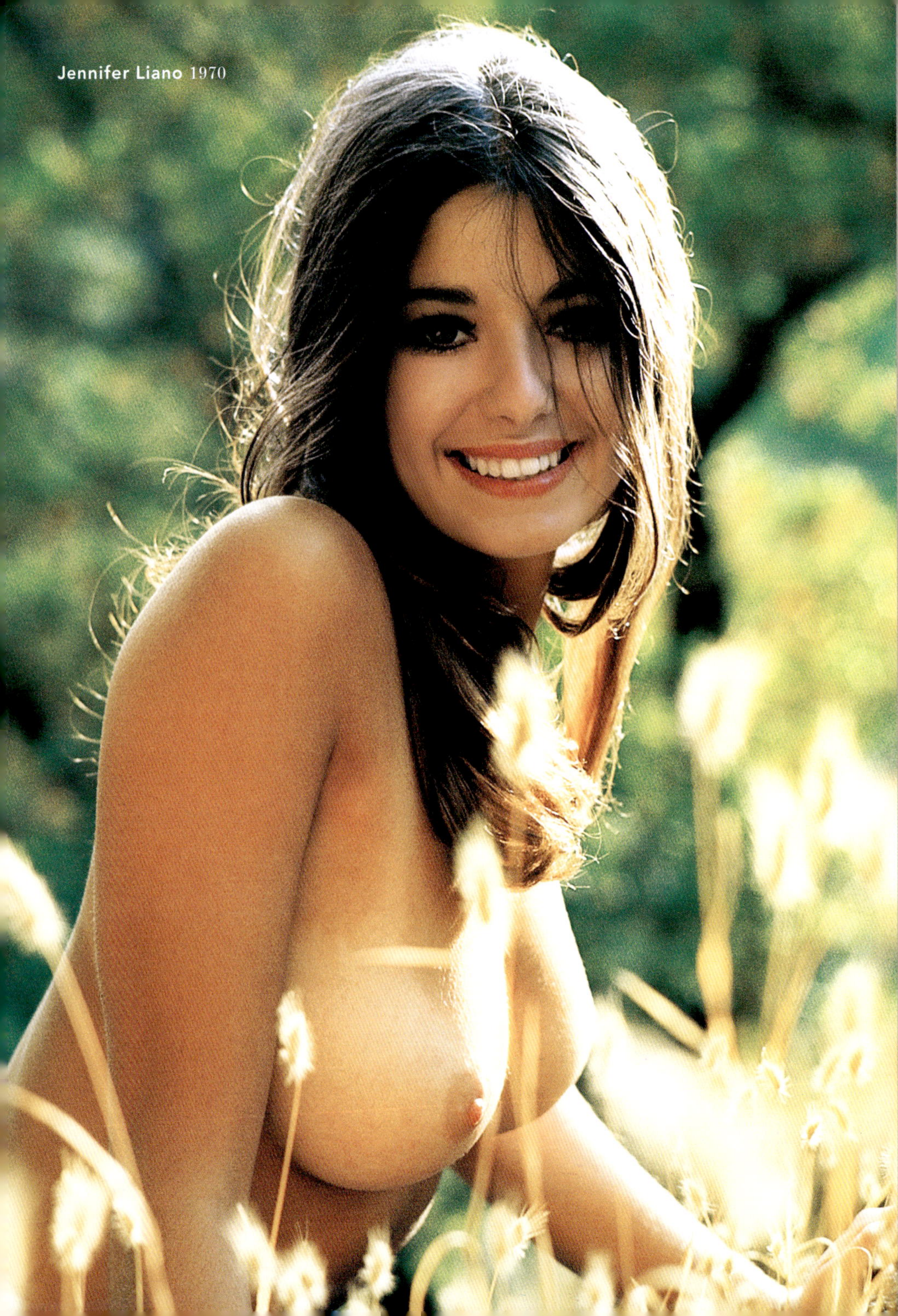

Jennifer Liano 1970

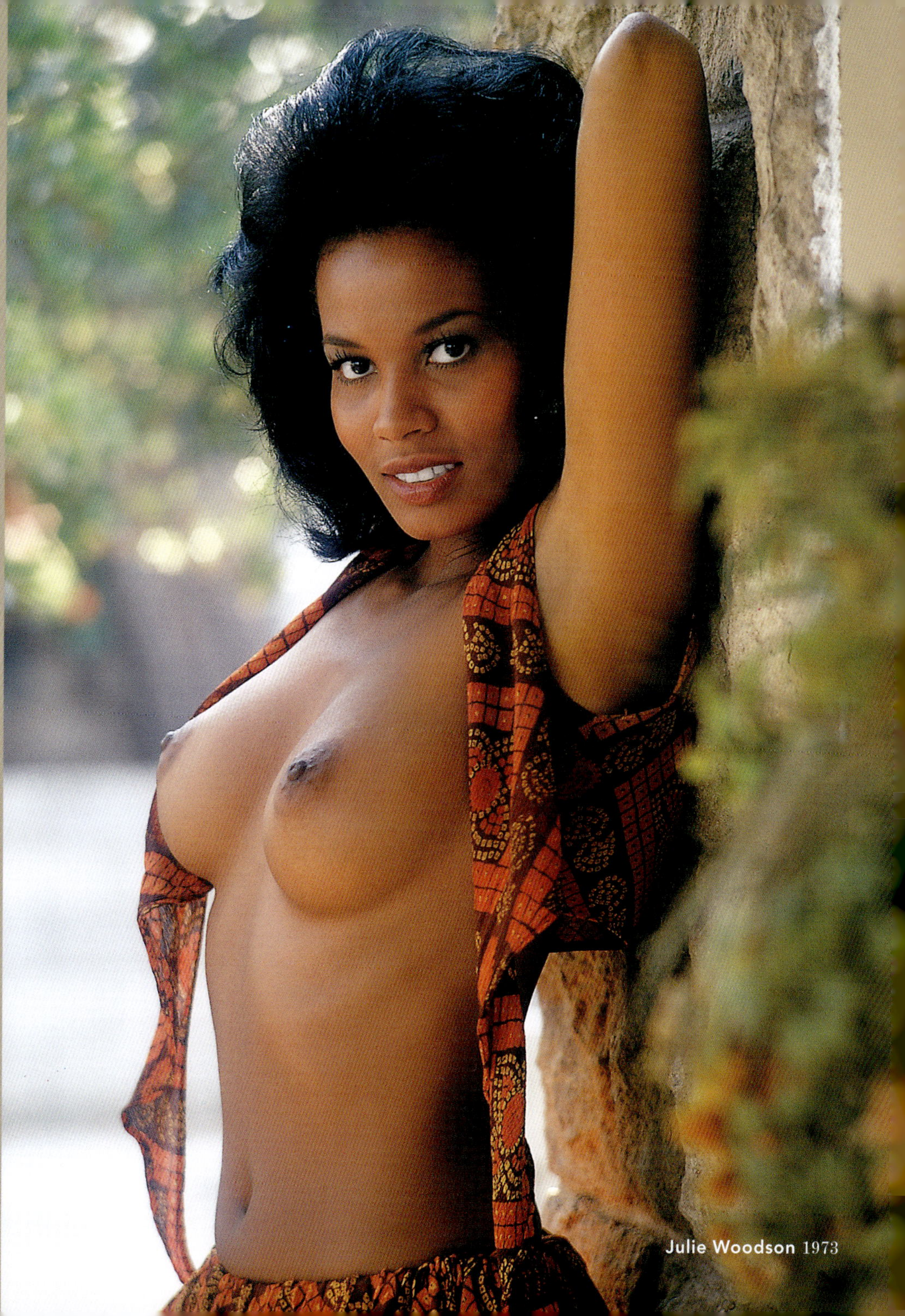

Julie Woodson 1973

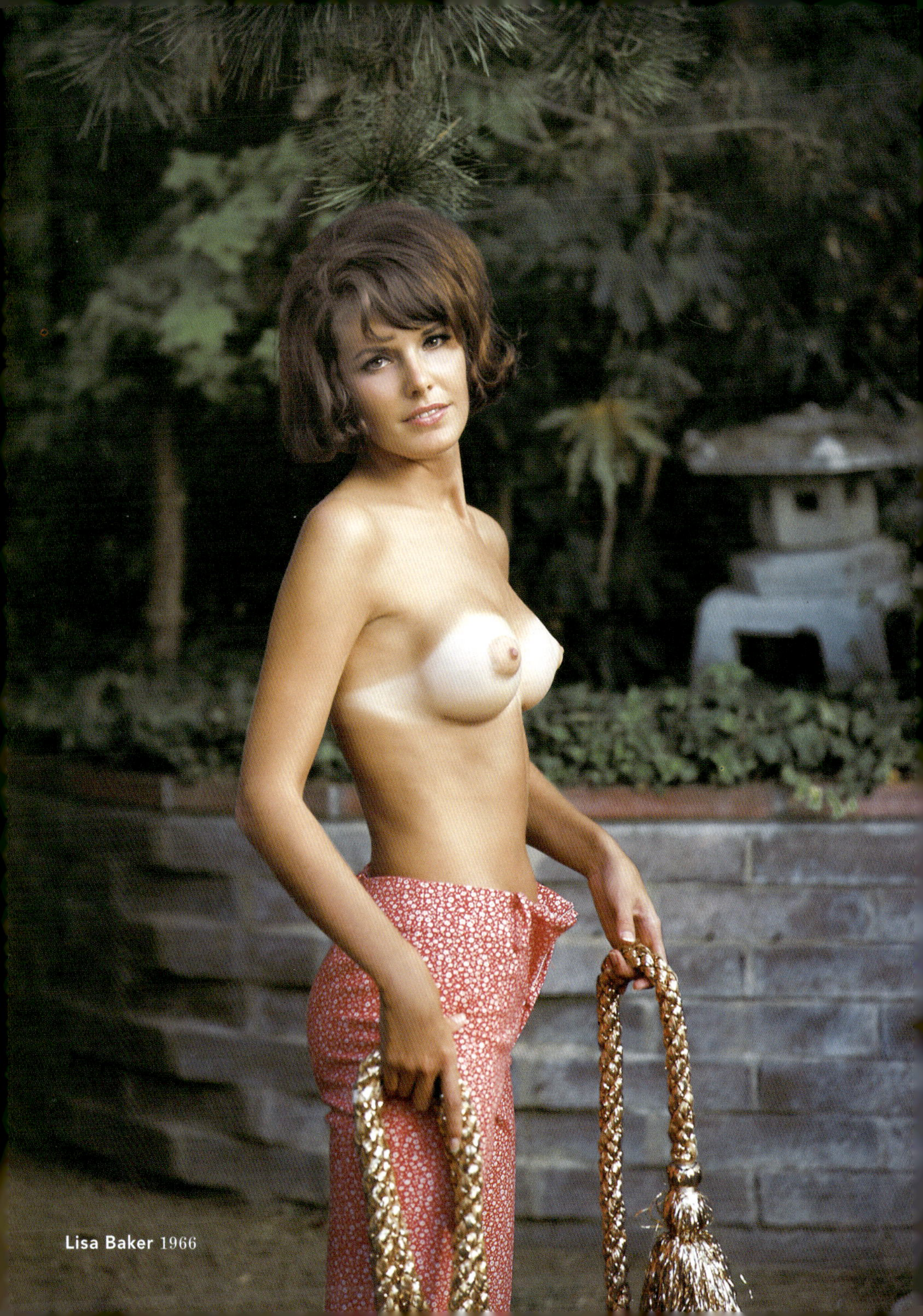

Lisa Baker 1966

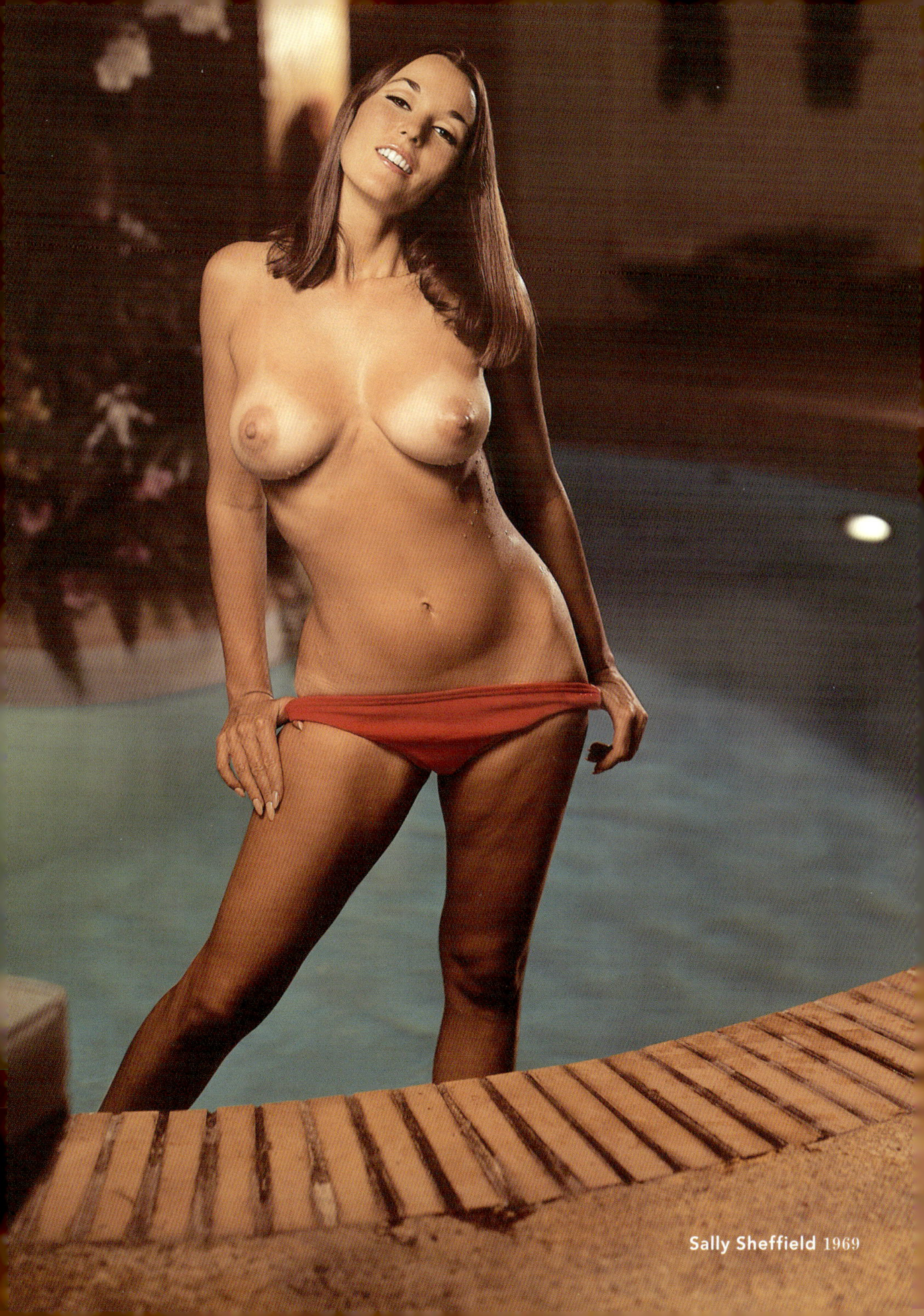

Sally Sheffield 1969

Jean Jani 1957

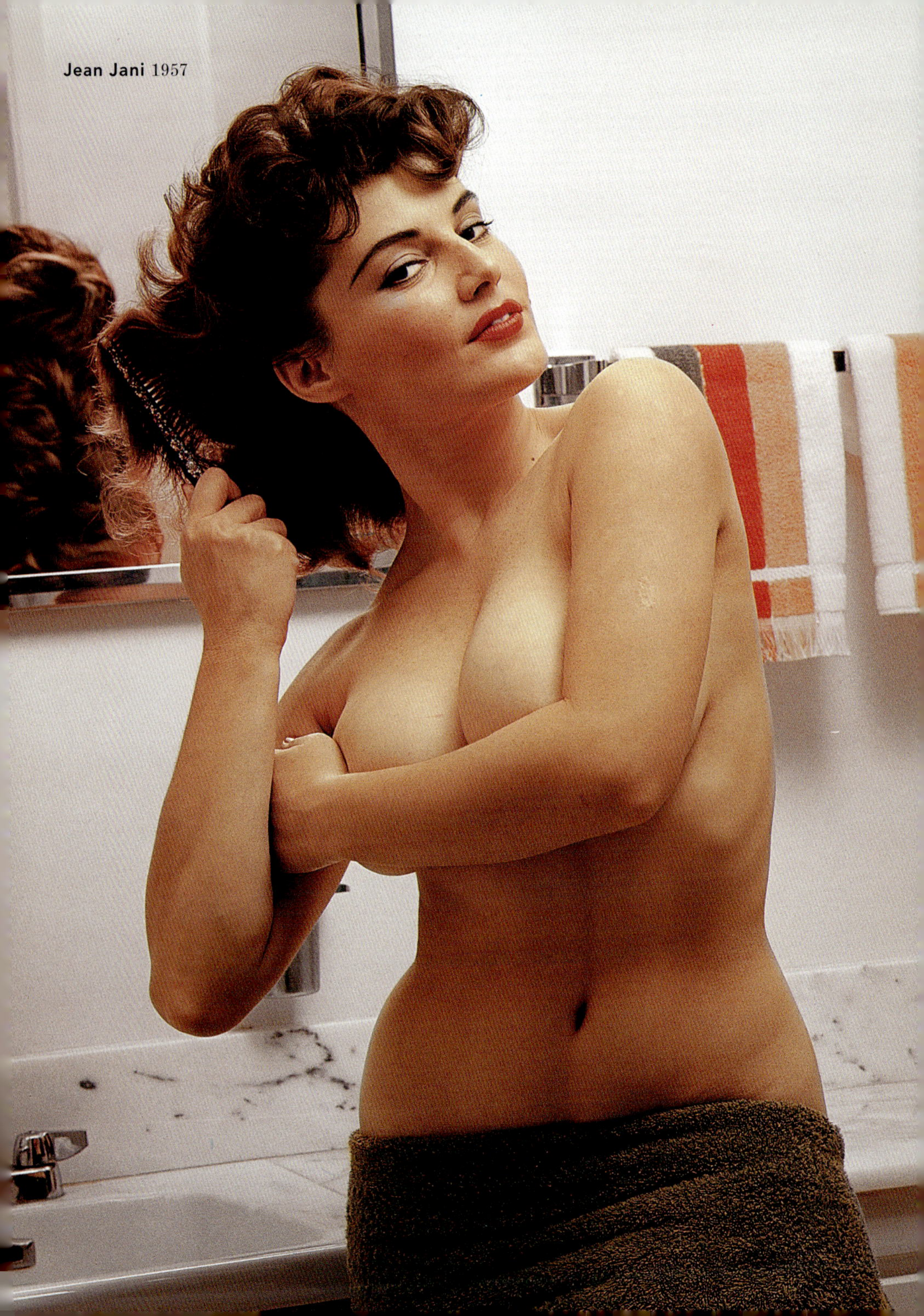

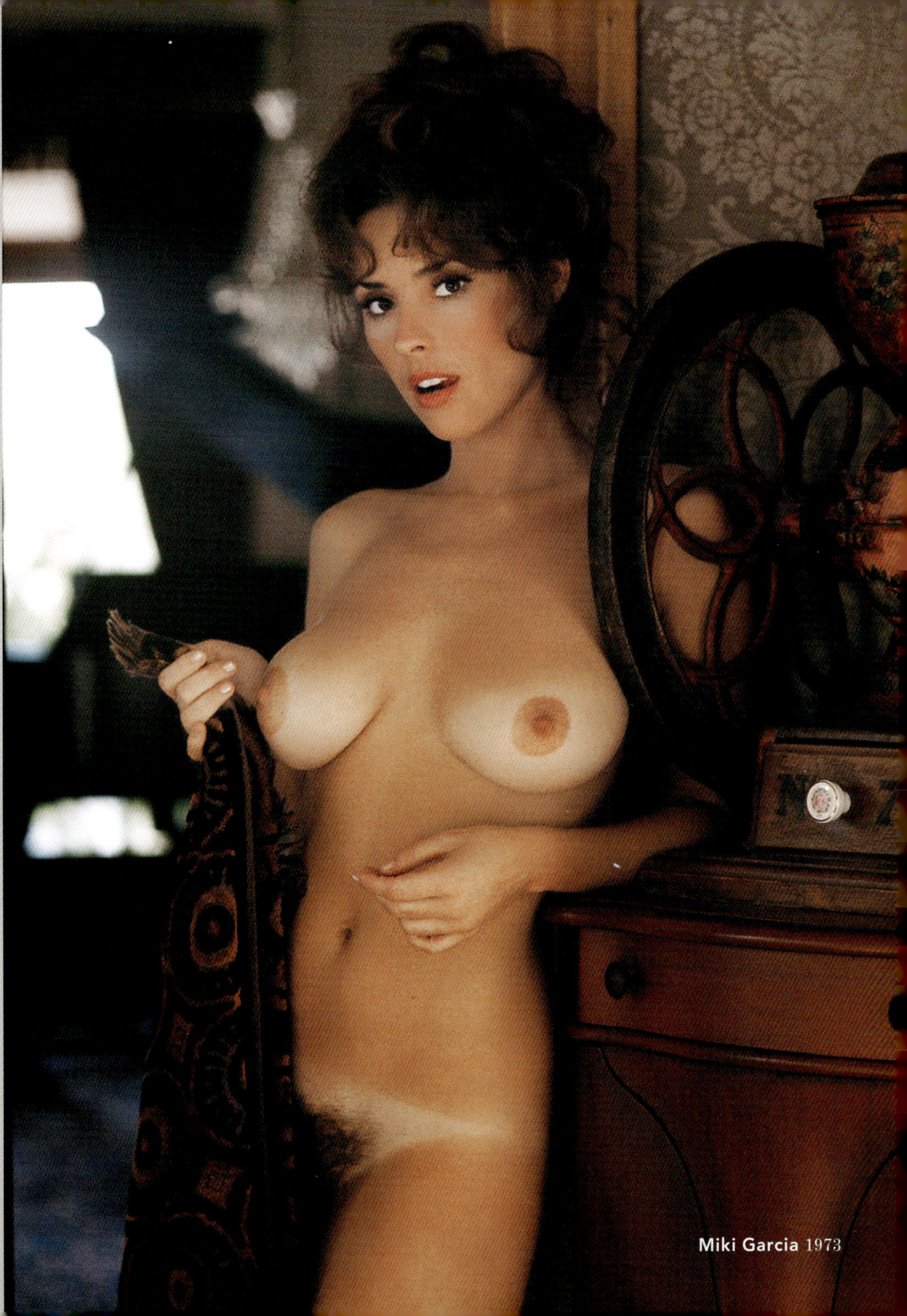

Miki Garcia 1973

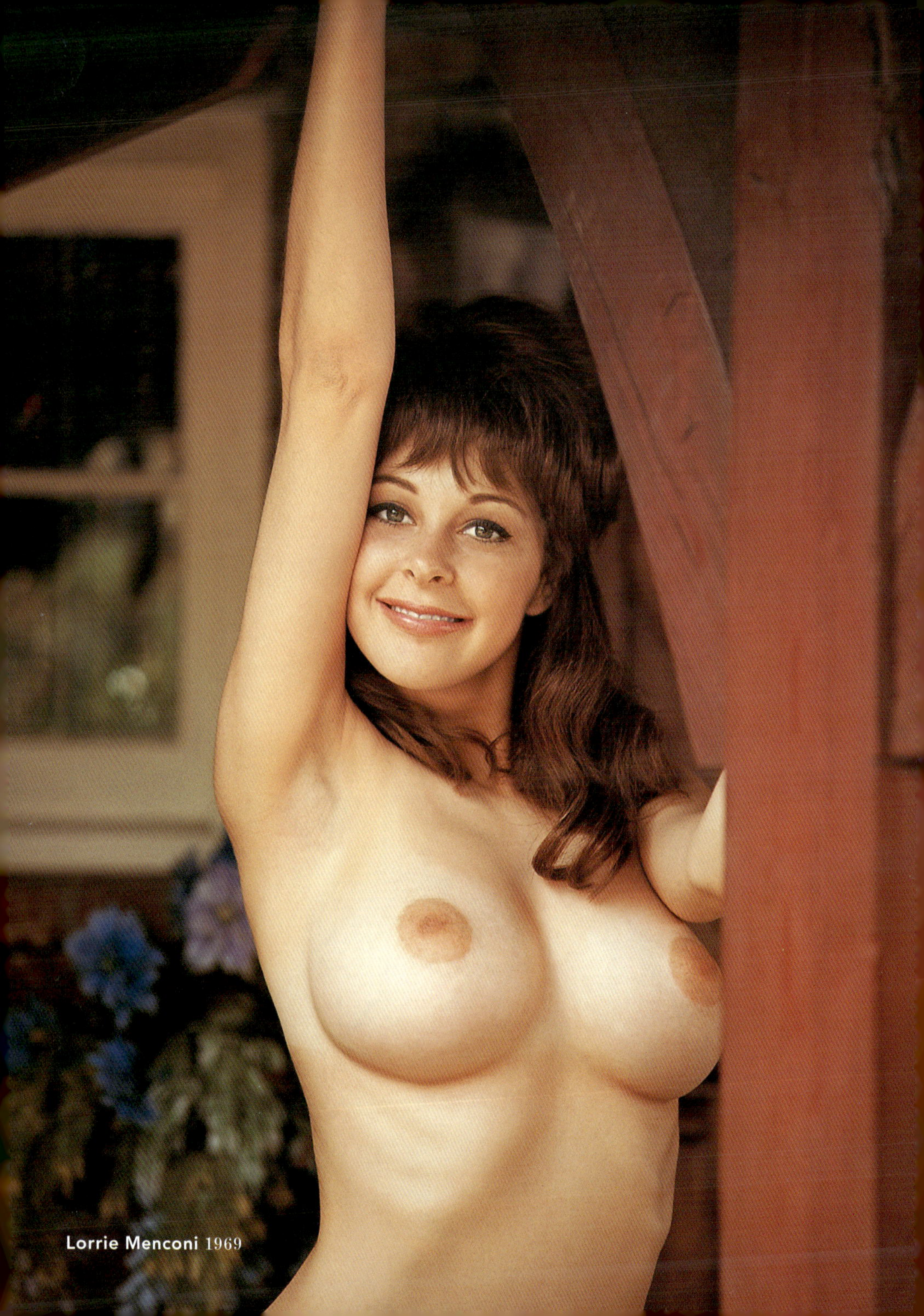

Lorrie Menconi 1969

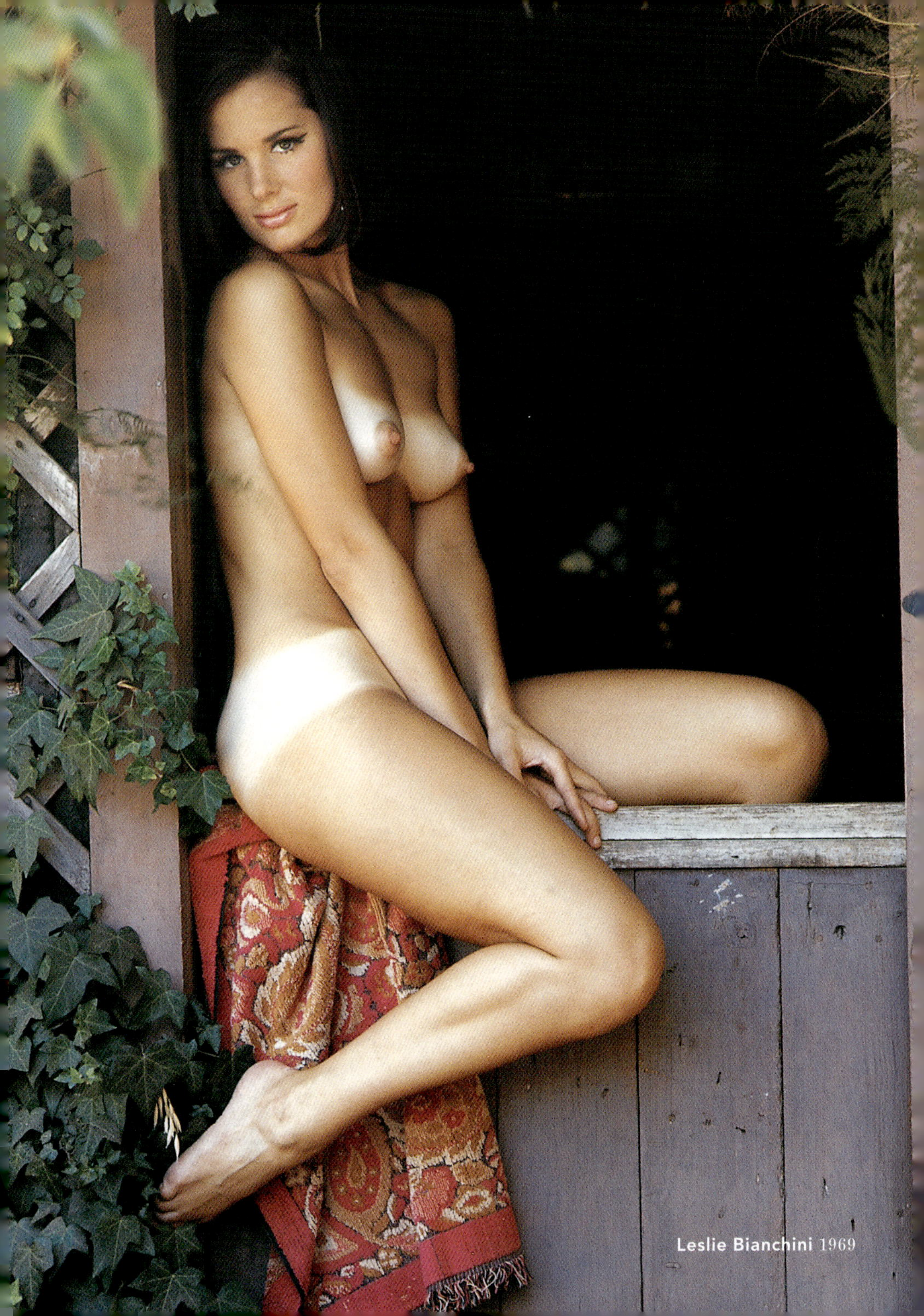

Leslie Bianchini 1969

China Lee 1964

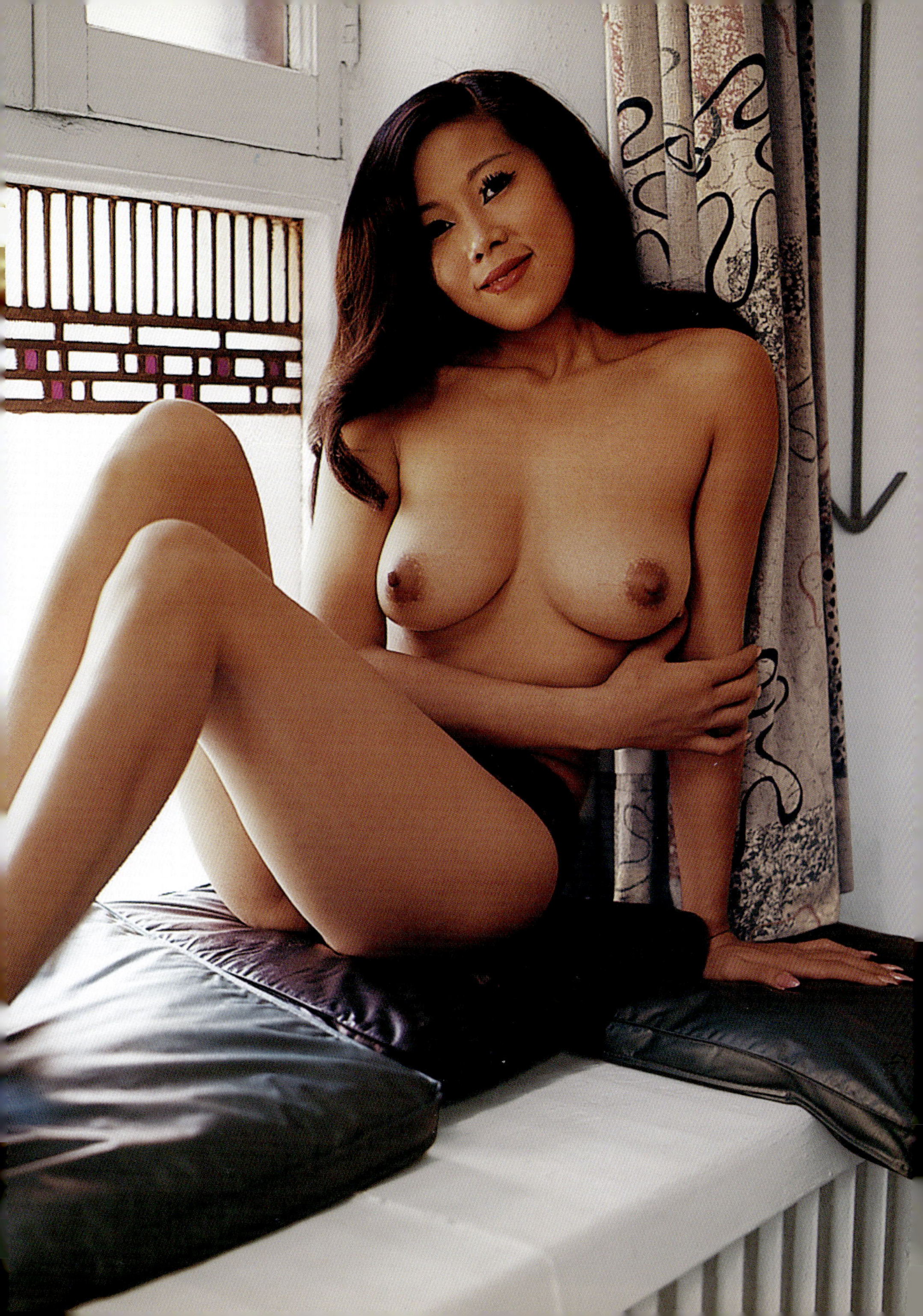

Clayre Peters 1959

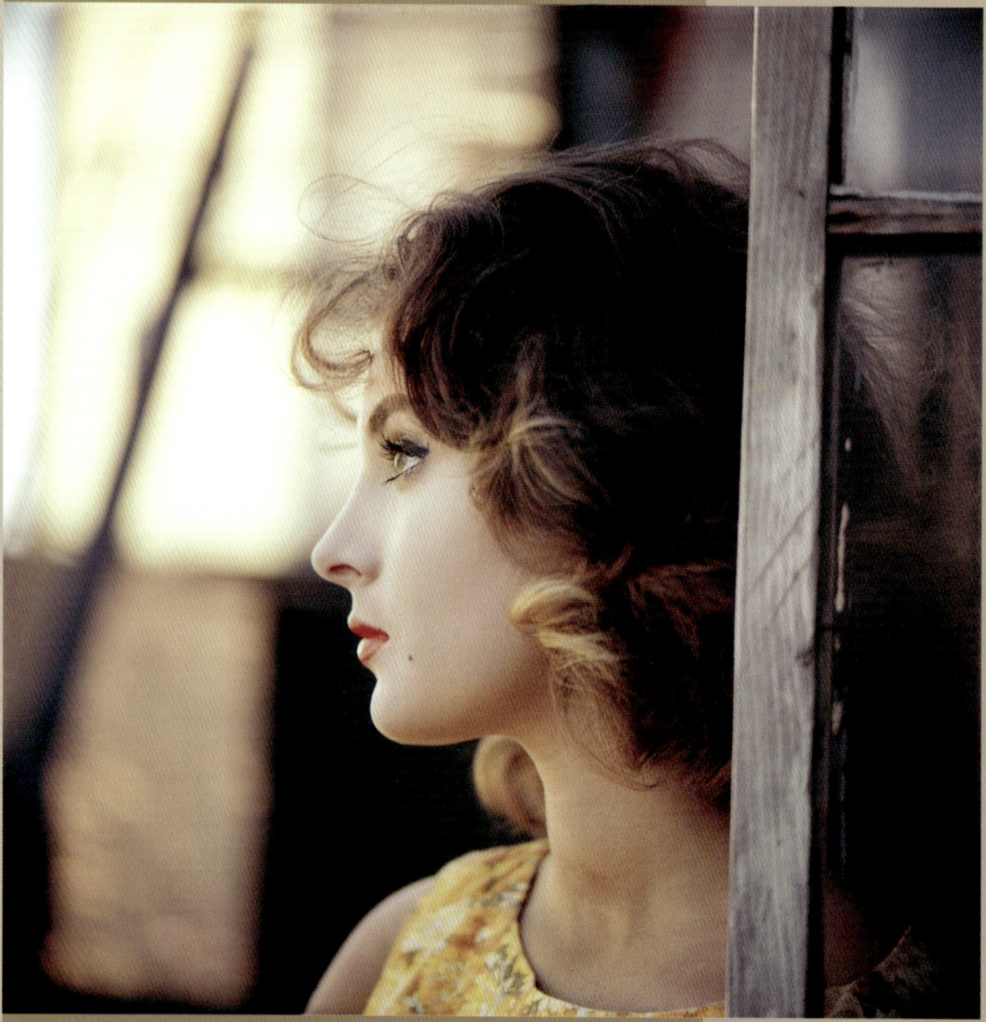

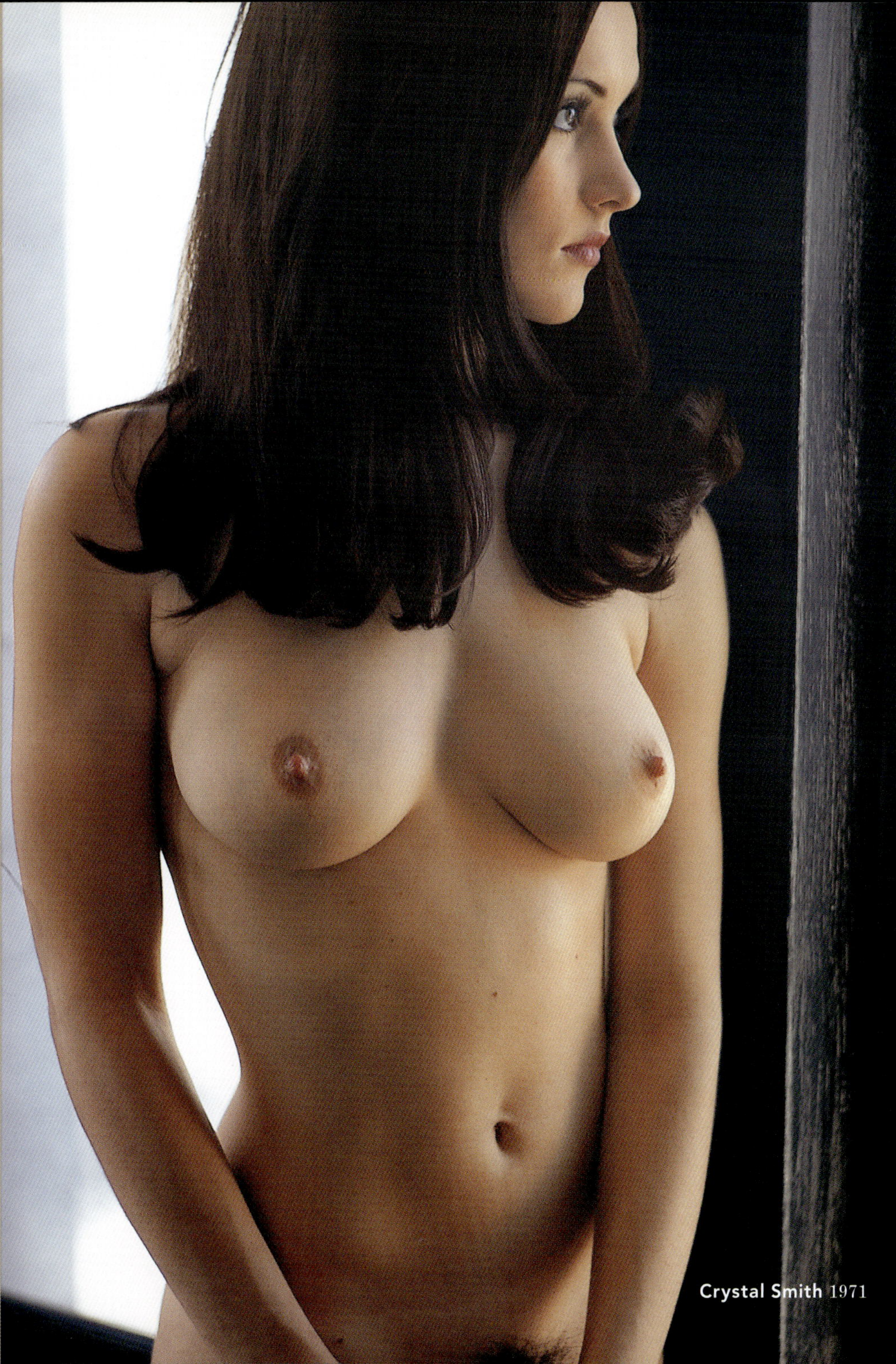

Crystal Smith 1971

"What do you care about a leggy brunette in nylons? Or did I just answer my own question?"

ZATANNA, IN *BATMAN: THE ANIMATED SERIES*

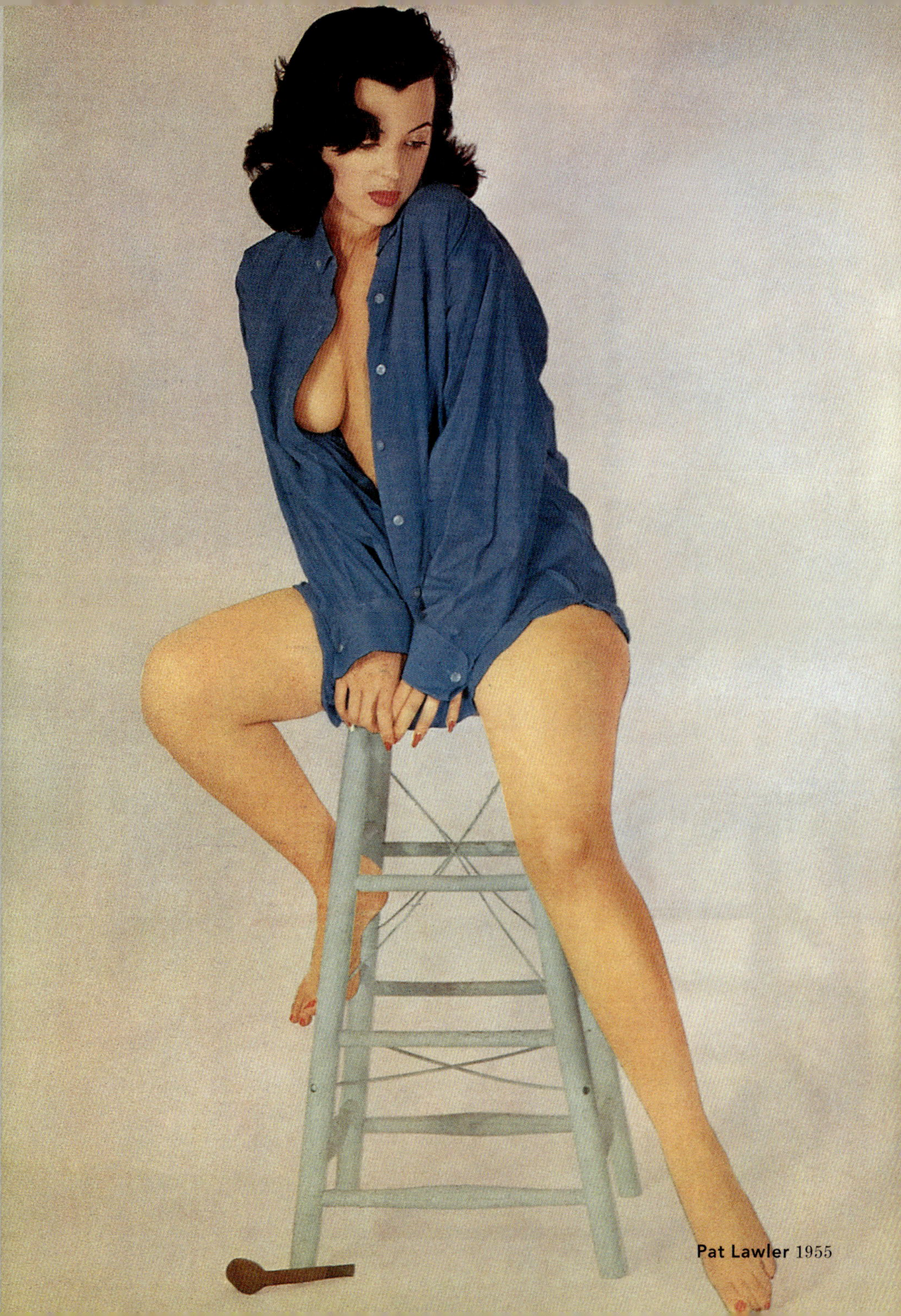

Pat Lawler 1955

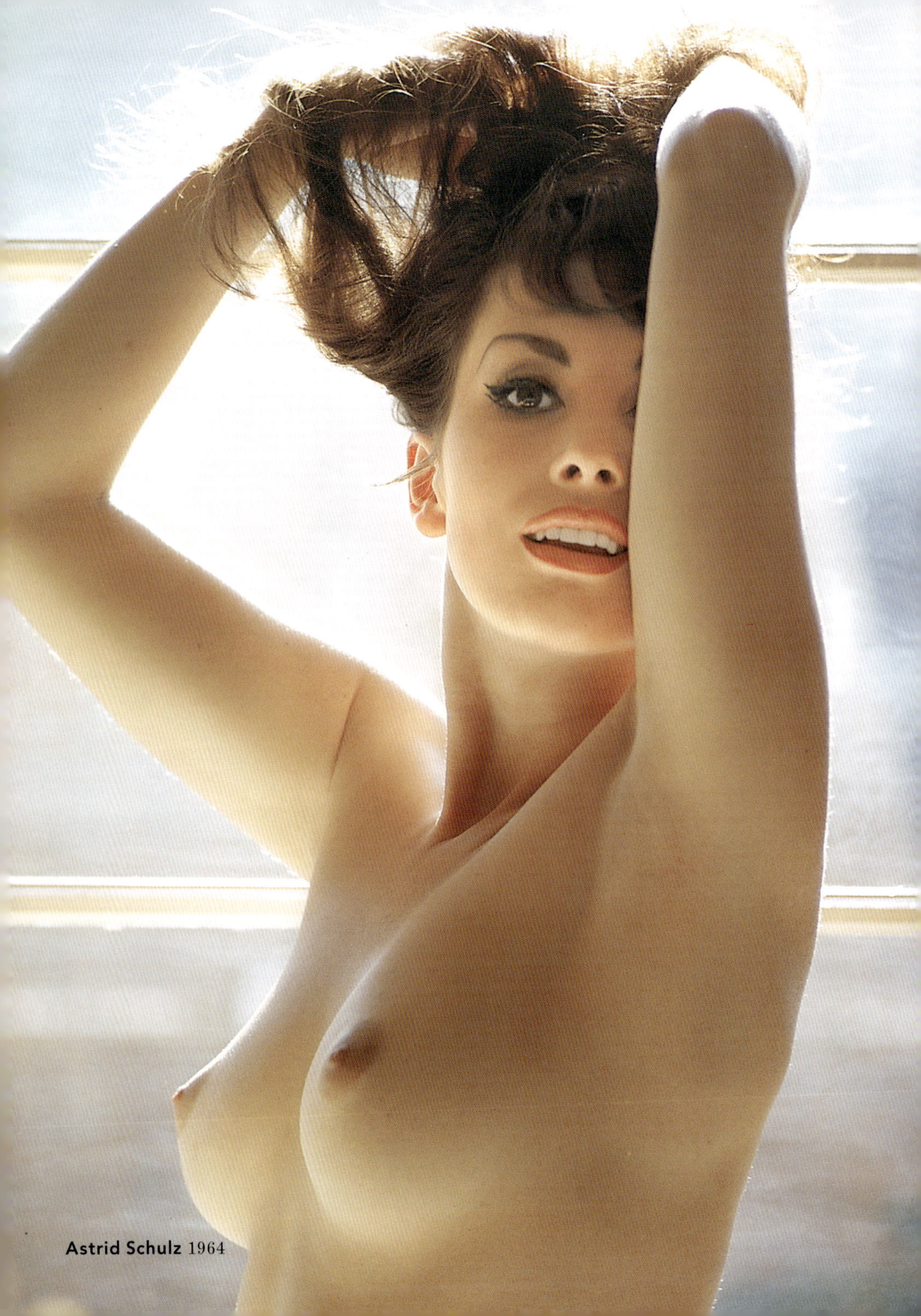

Astrid Schulz 1964

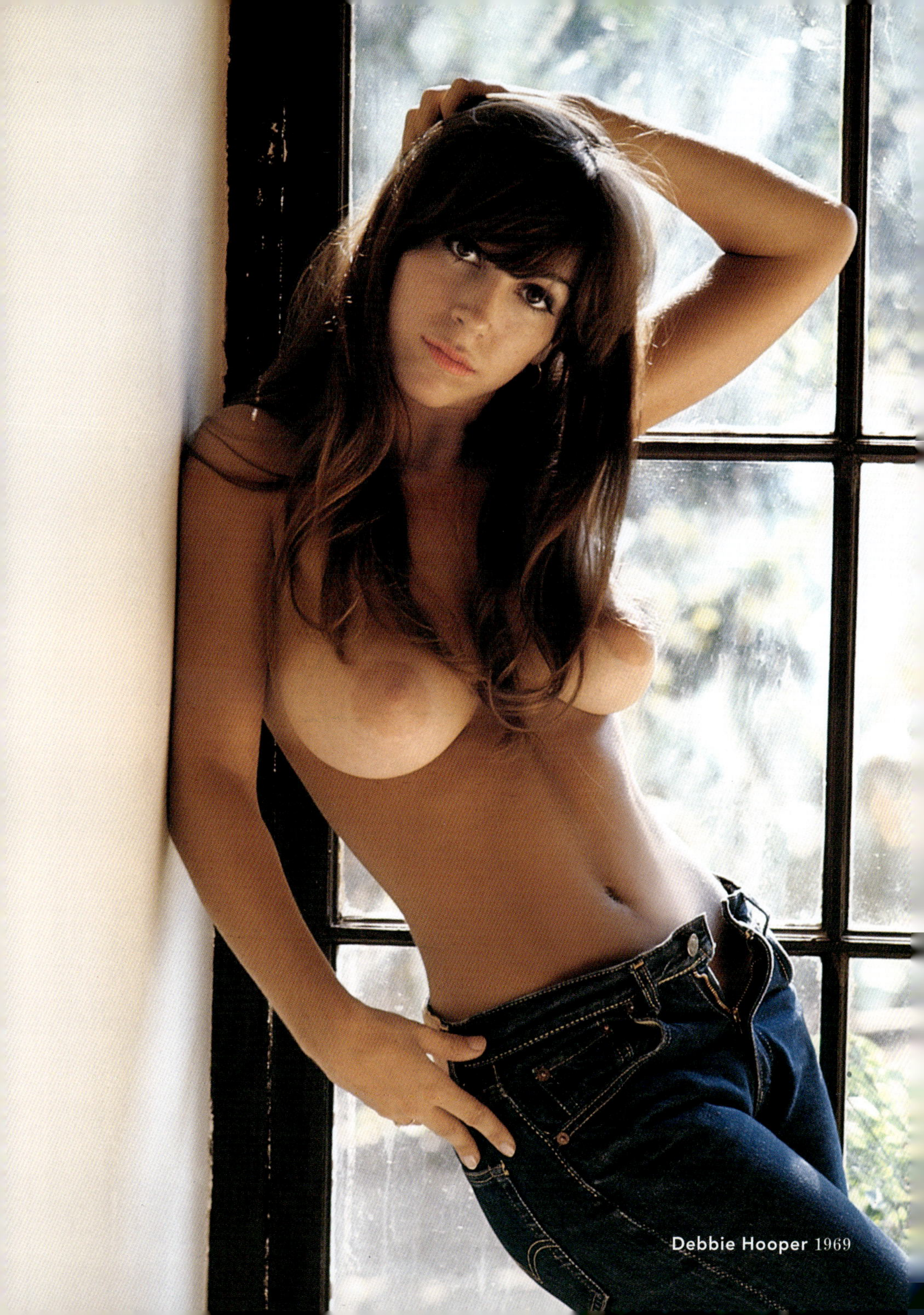

Debbie Hooper 1969

"I . . . am small, like the wren, and
my hair is bold like the chestnut burr;
and my eyes like the sherry in
the glass that the guest leaves."

EMILY DICKINSON

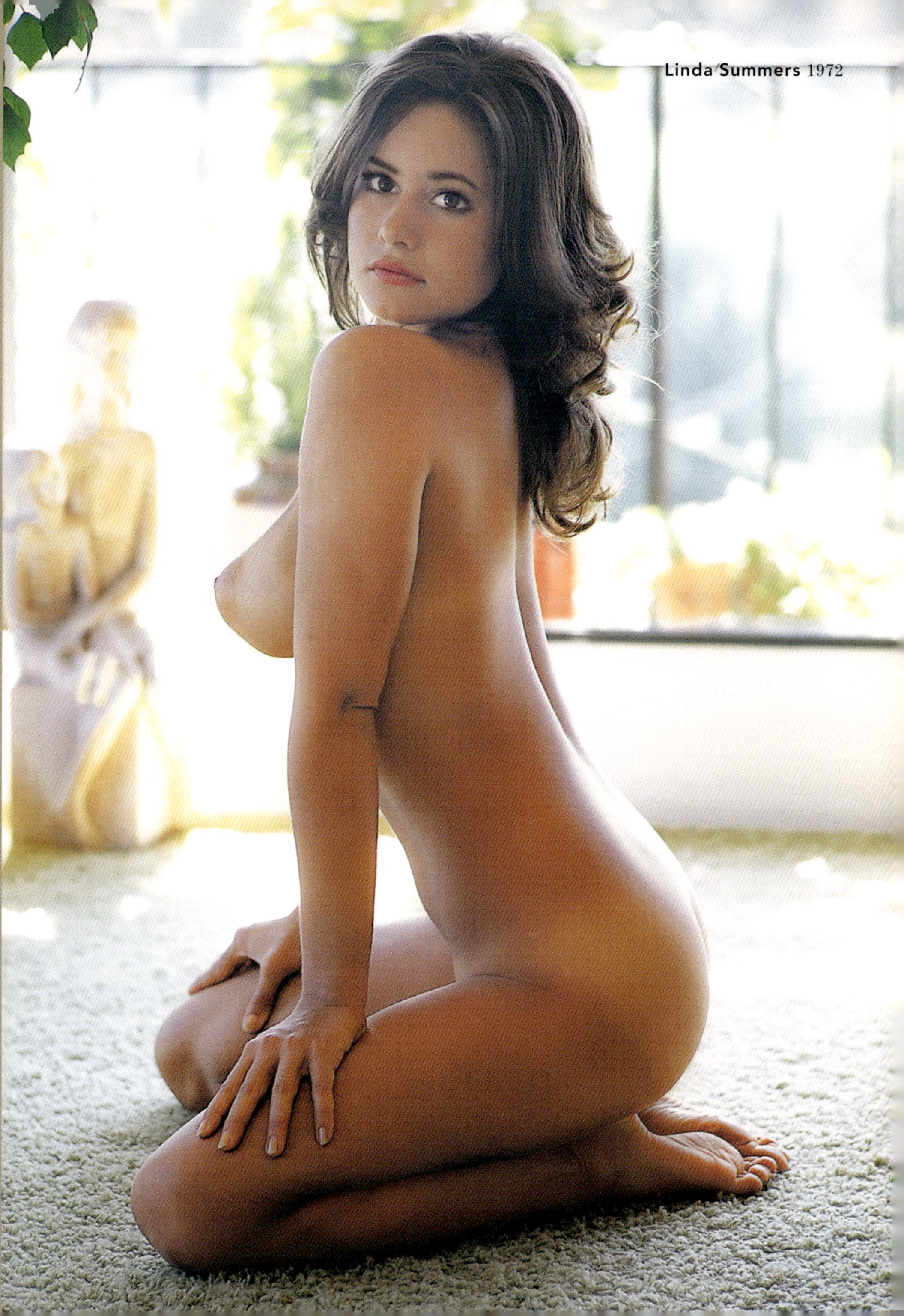
Linda Summers 1972

Anne Fleming 1955

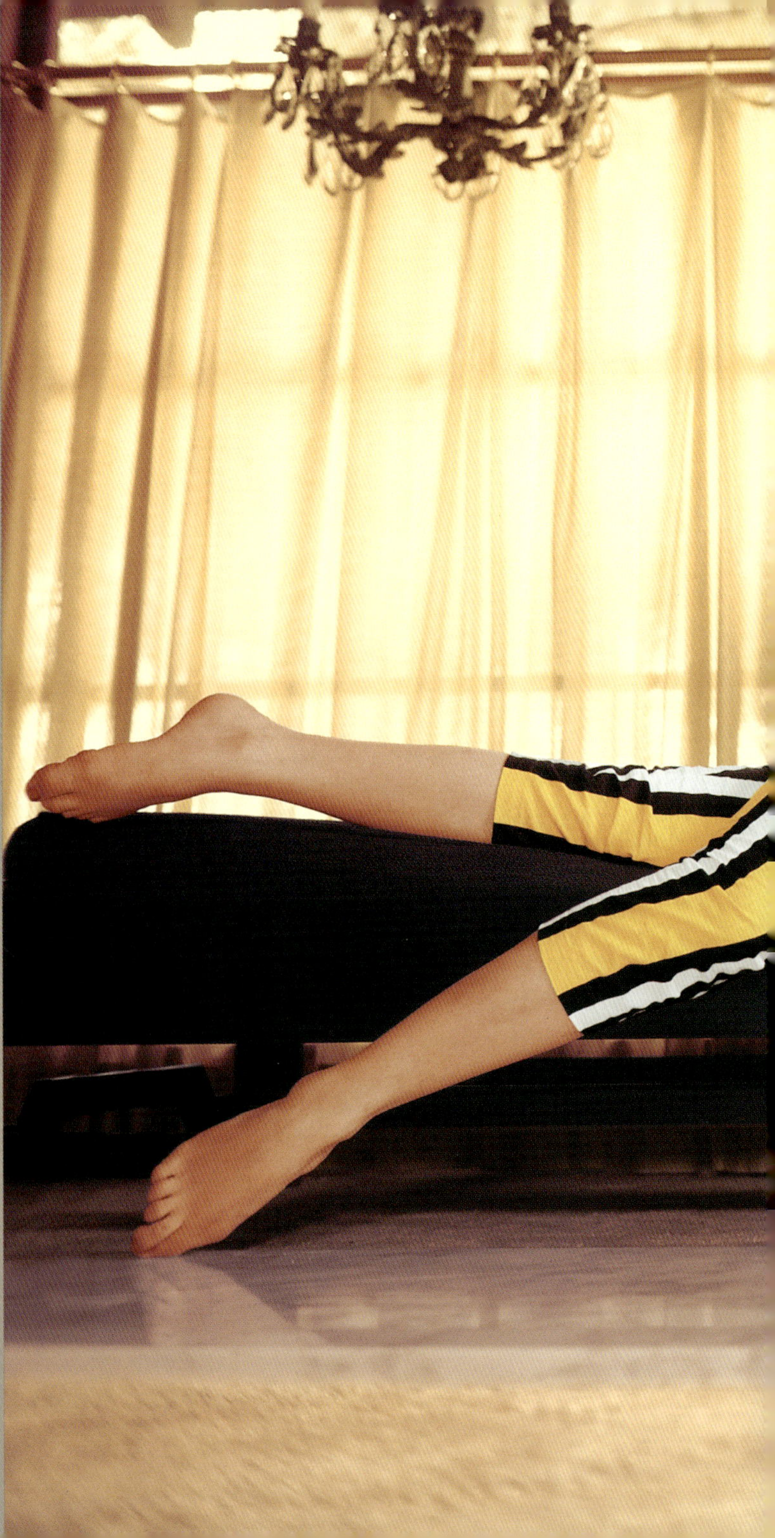

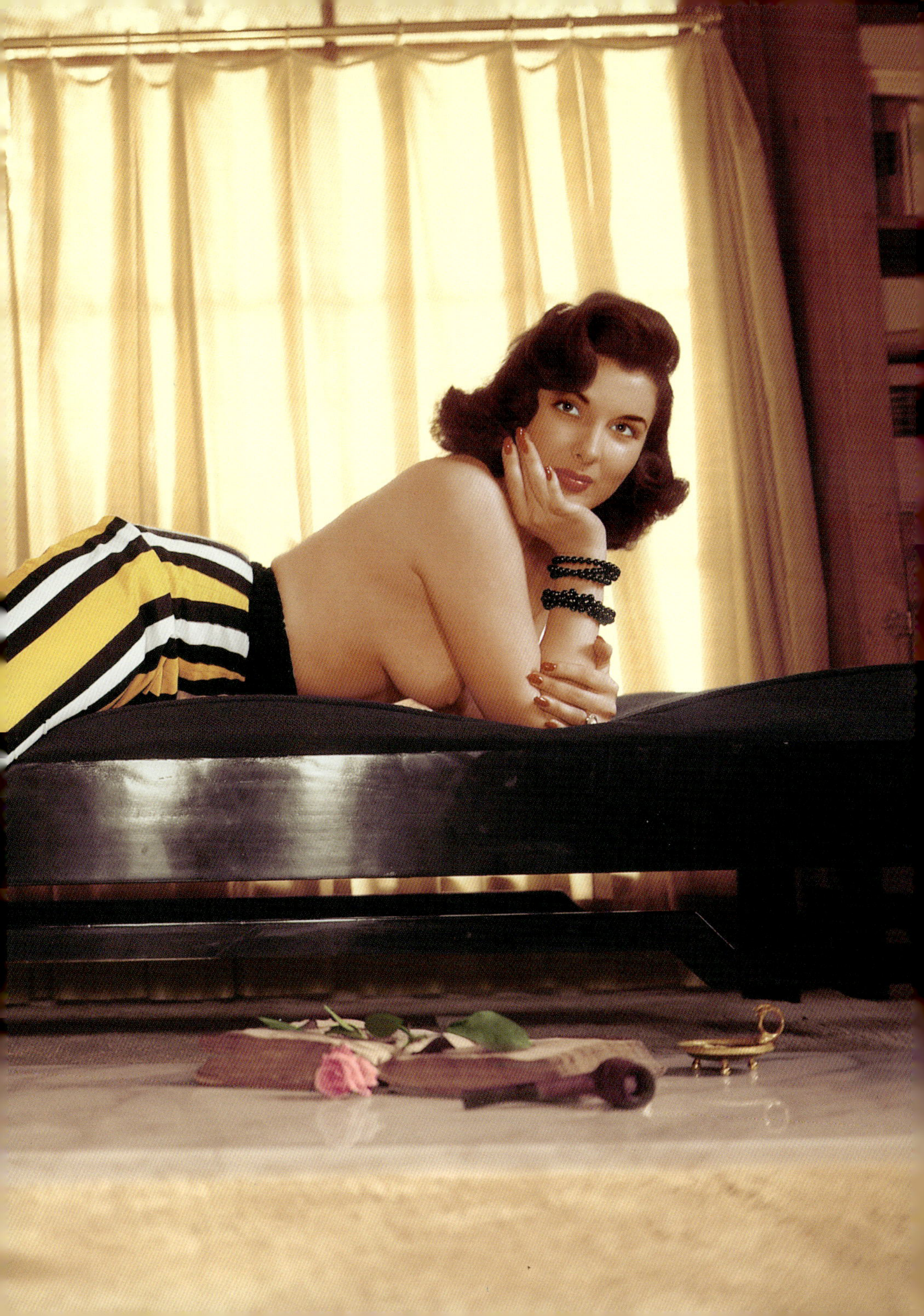

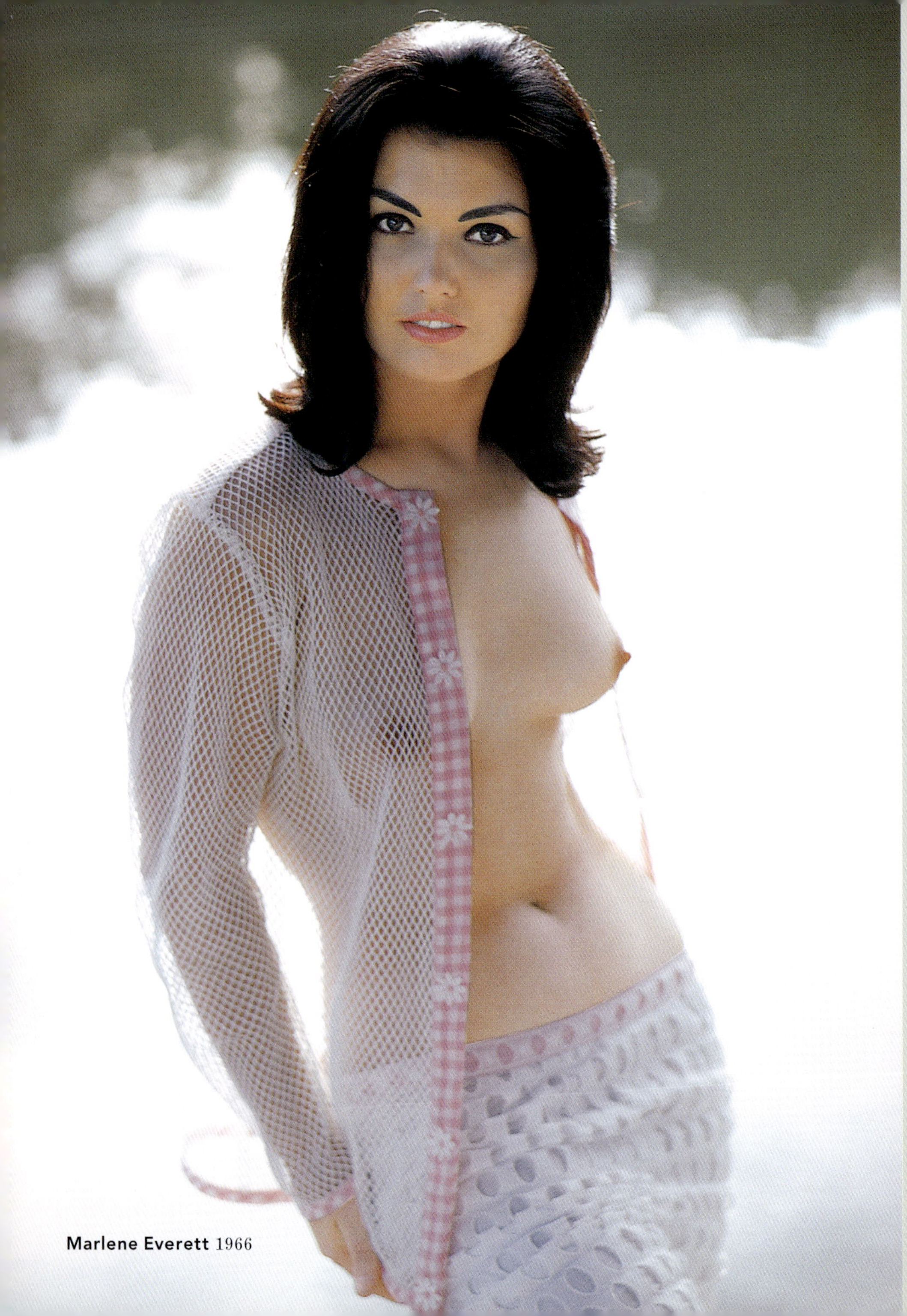

Marlene Everett 1966

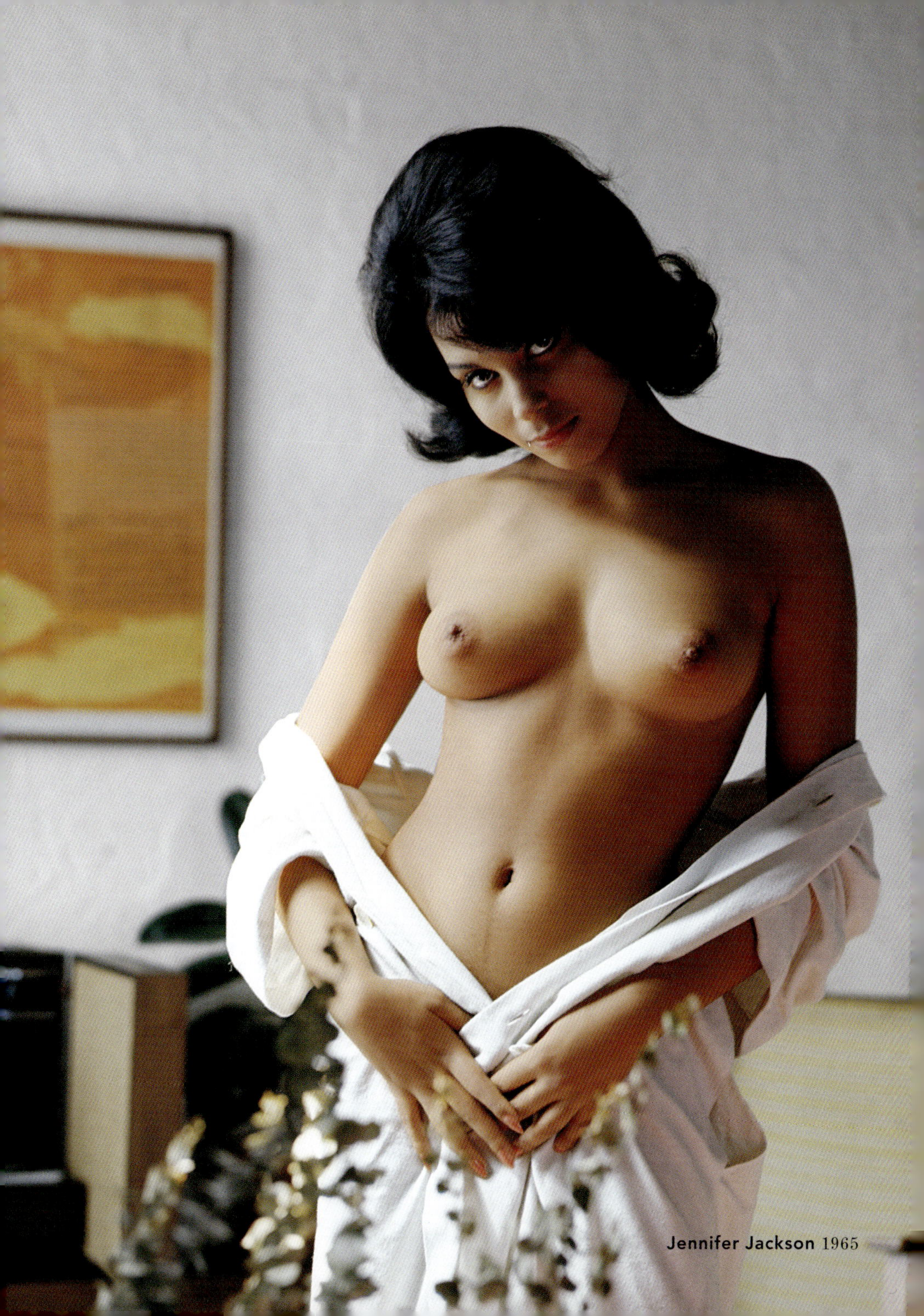

Jennifer Jackson 1965

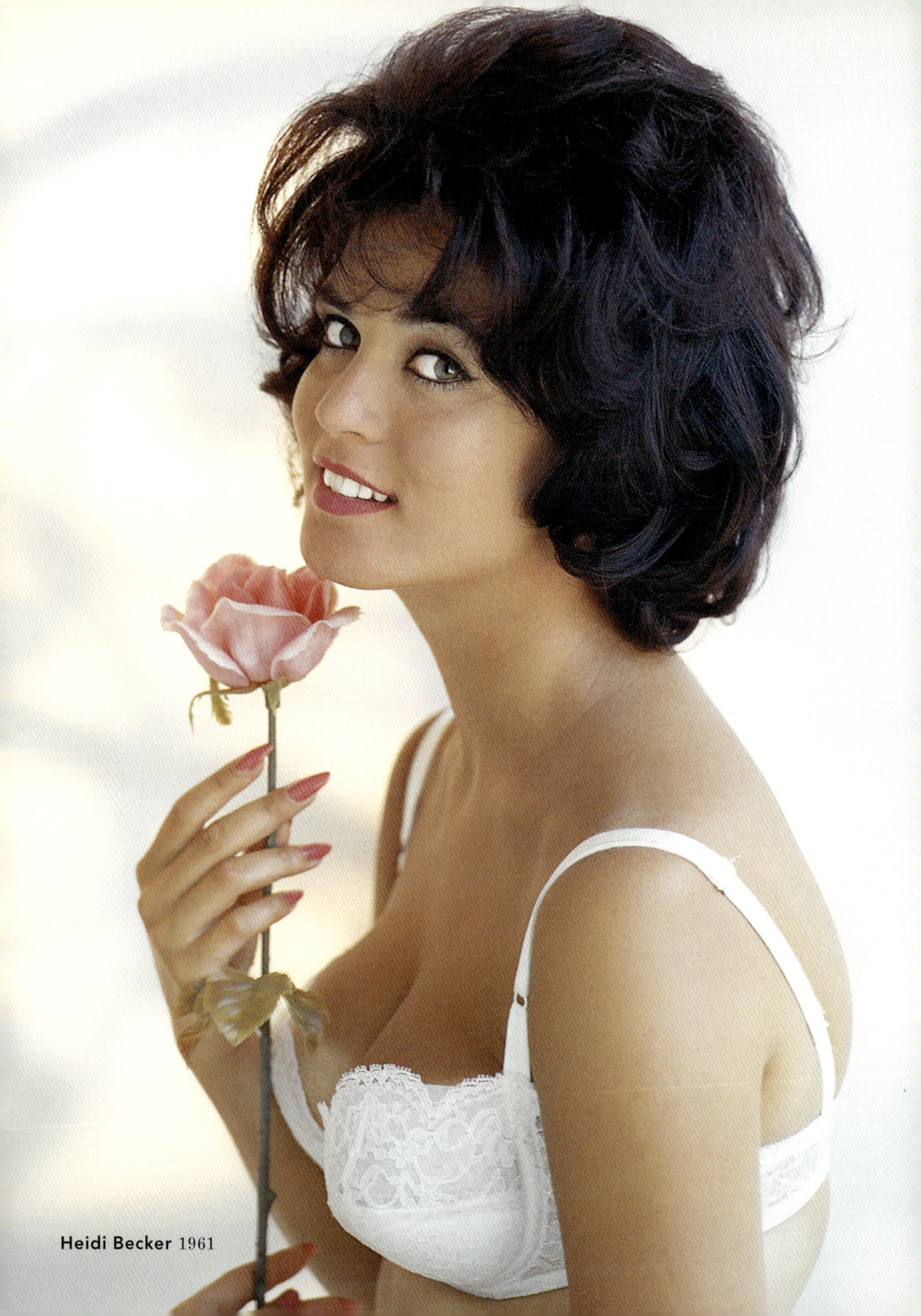

Heidi Becker 1961

"Gentlemen prefer blondes,
but marry brunettes."

ANITA LOOS

Jean Bell 1969

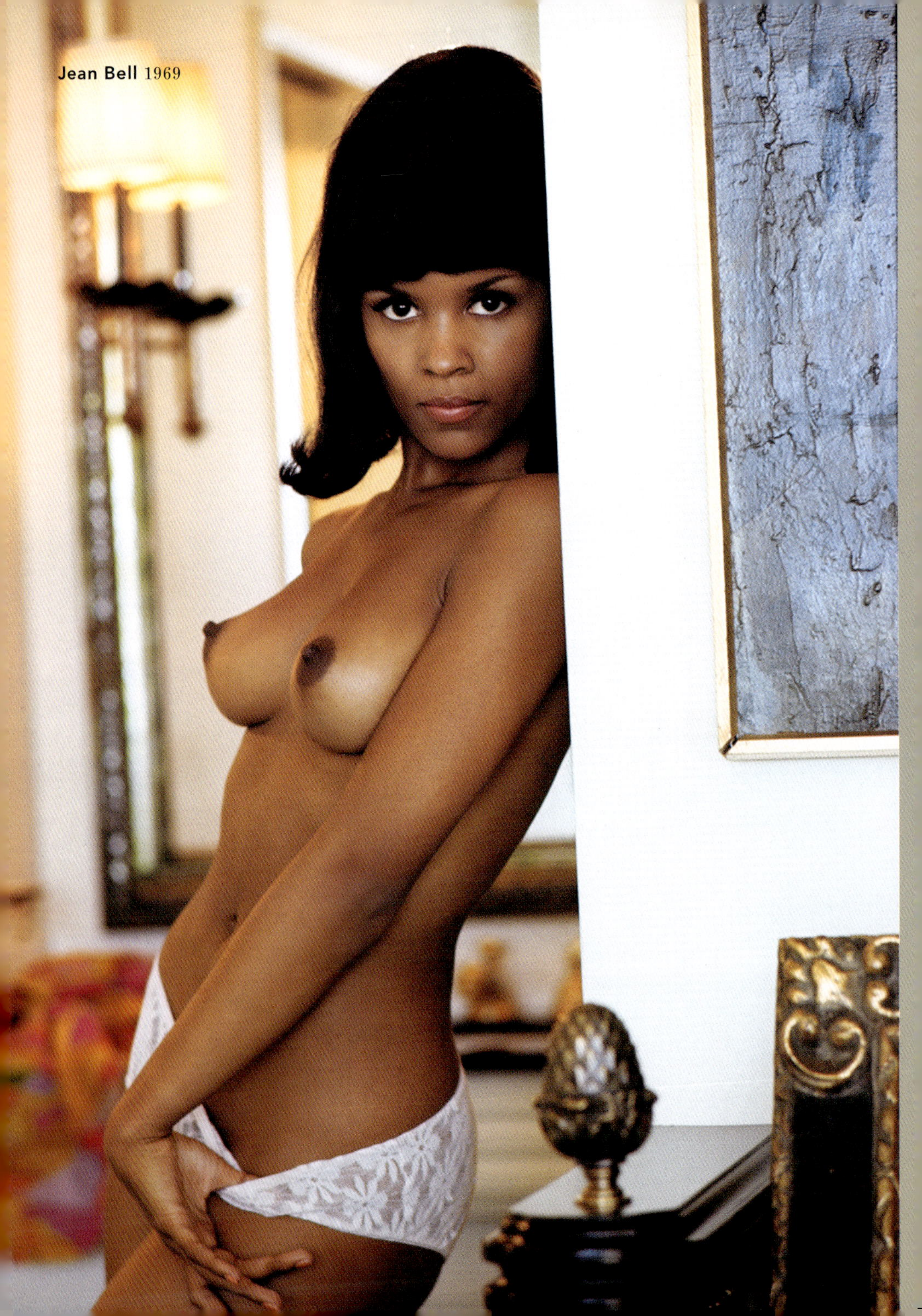

Karla Conway 1966

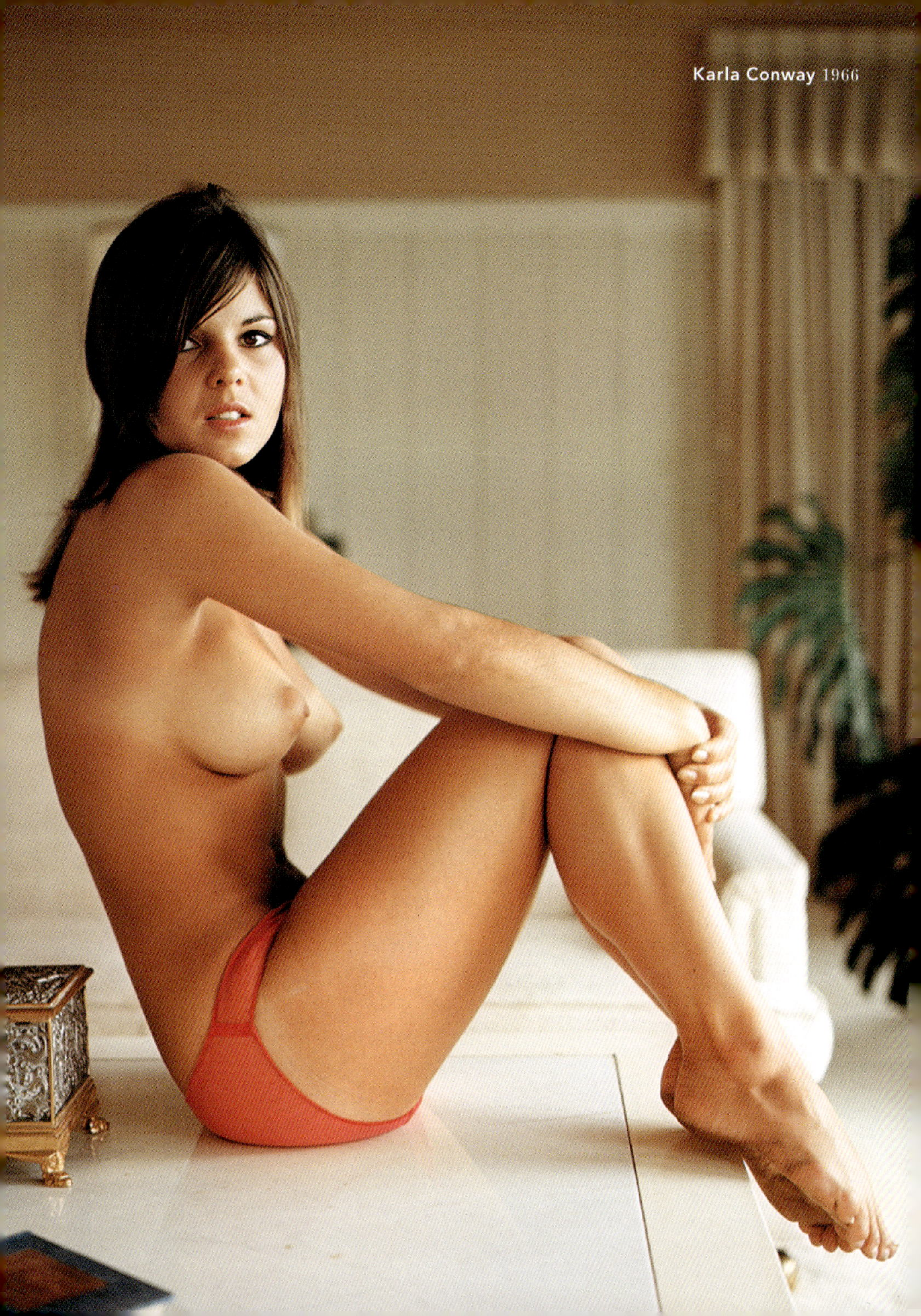

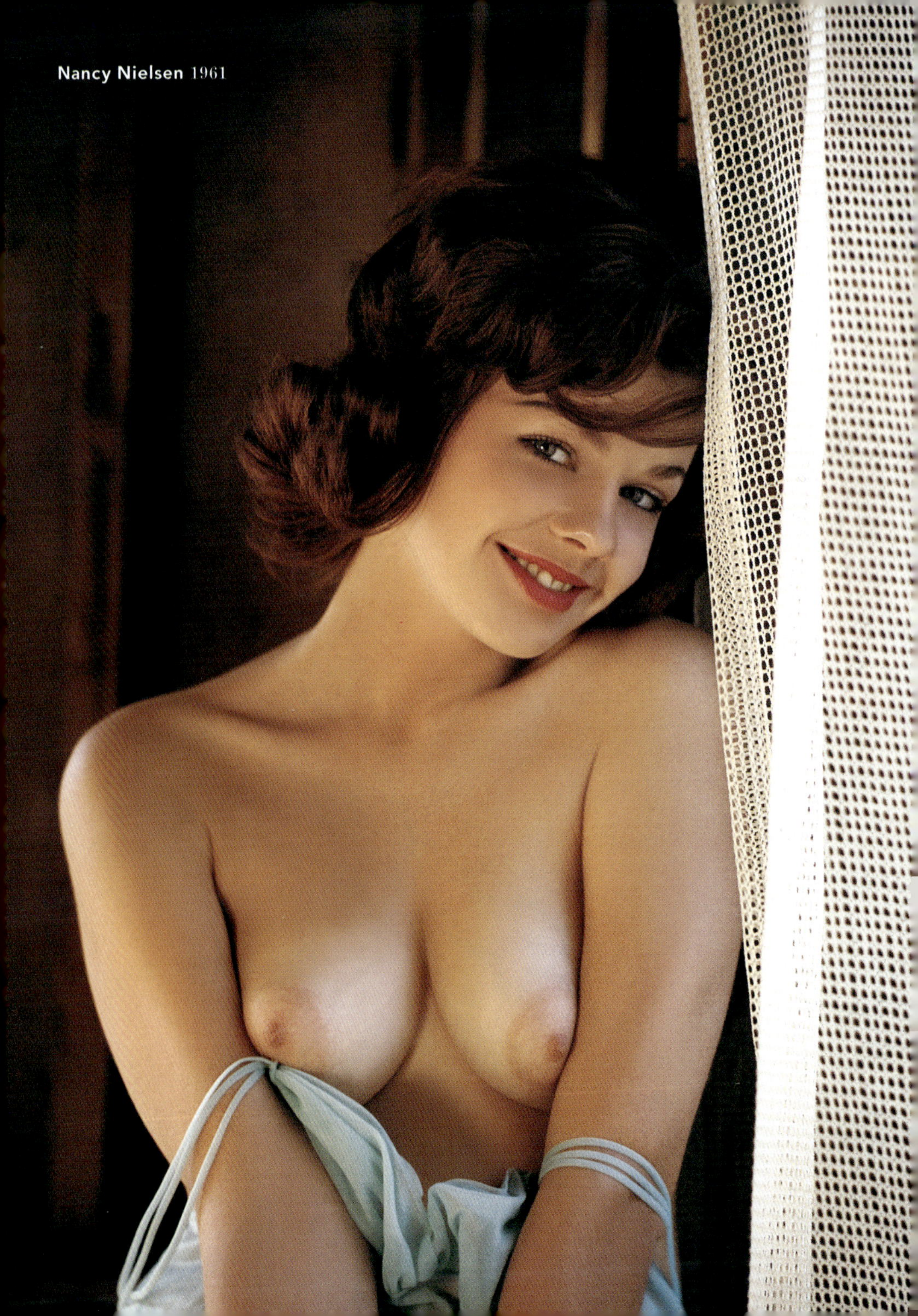

Nancy Nielsen 1961

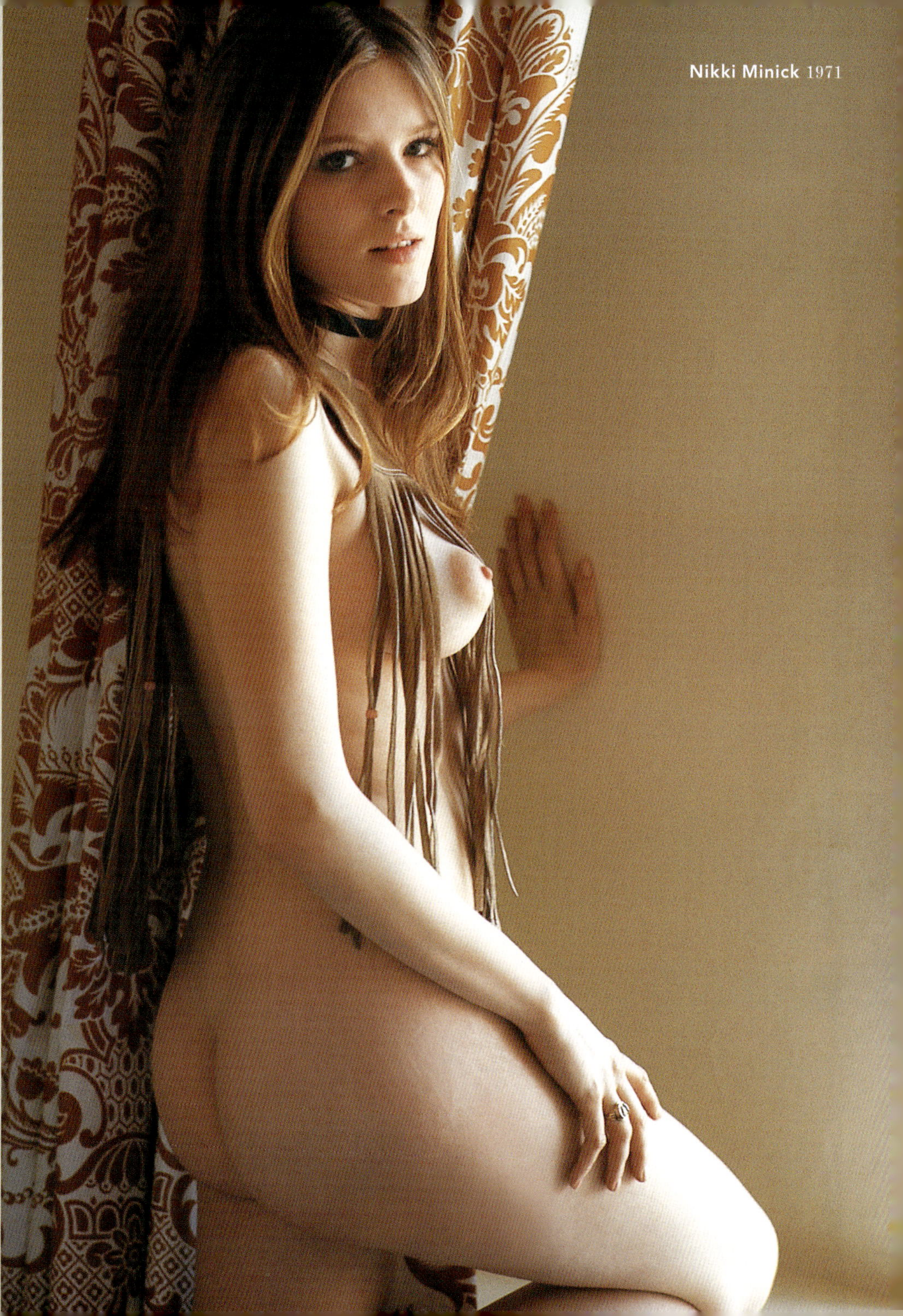

Nikki Minick 1971

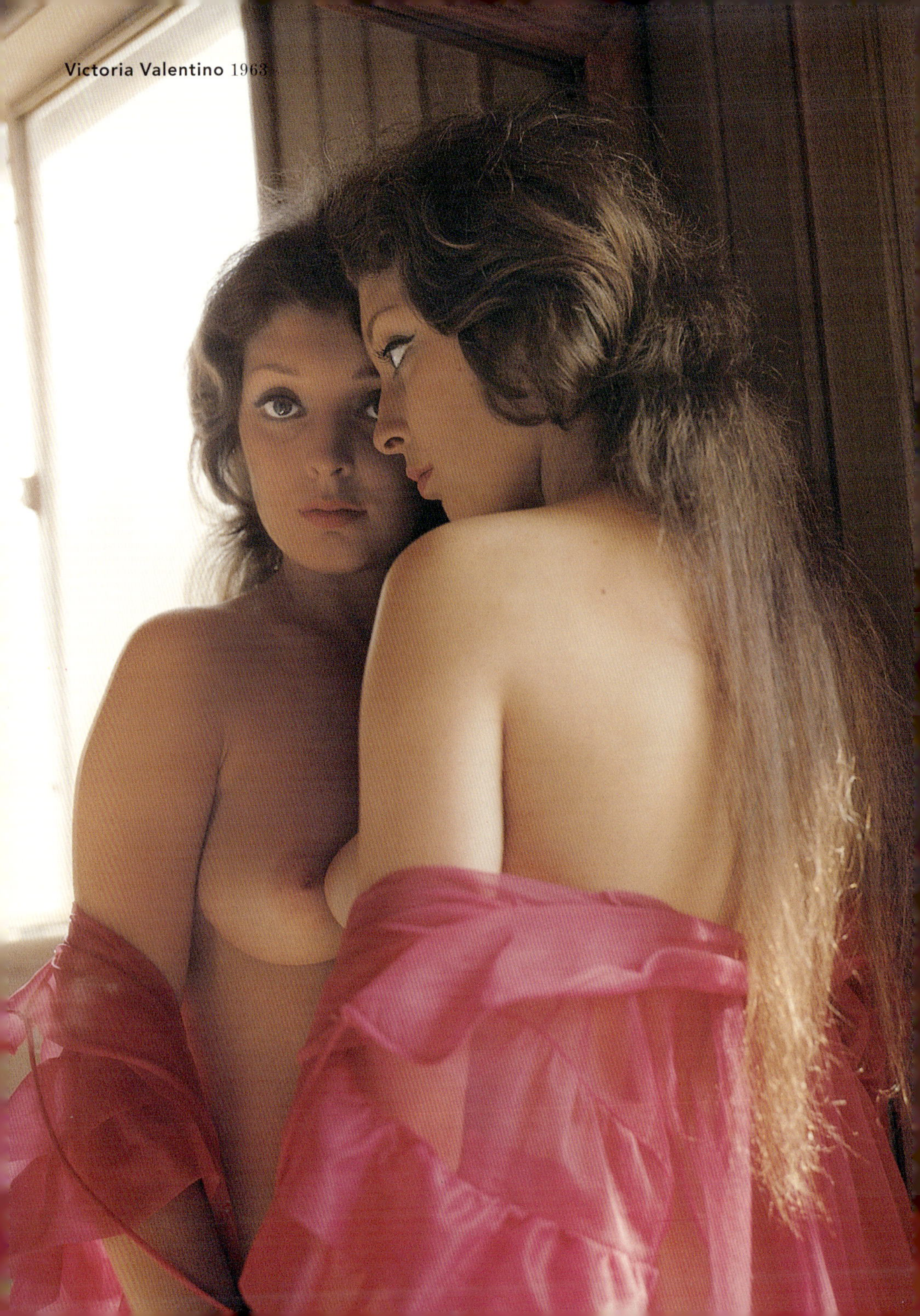

Victoria Valentino 1963

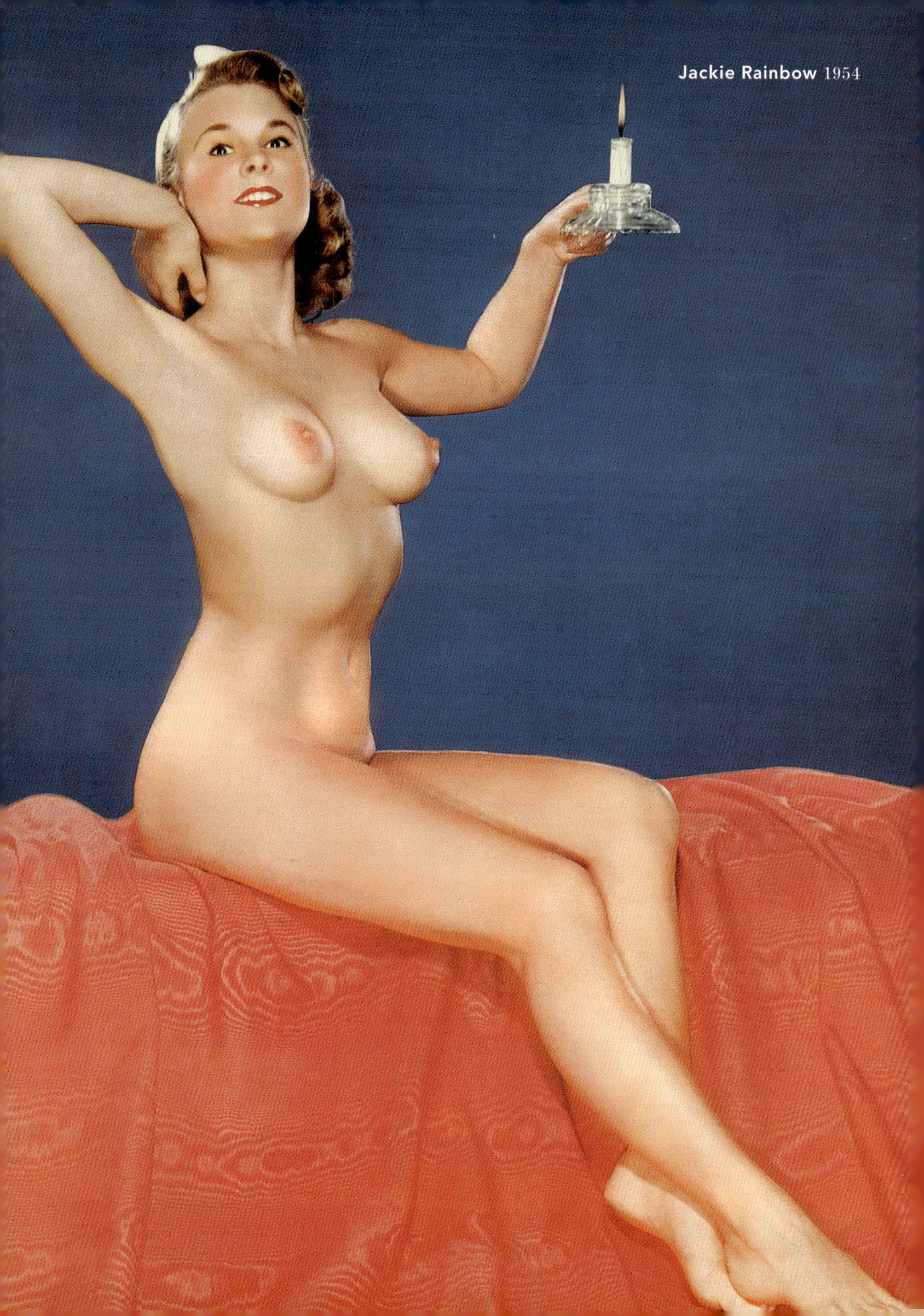

Jackie Rainbow 1954

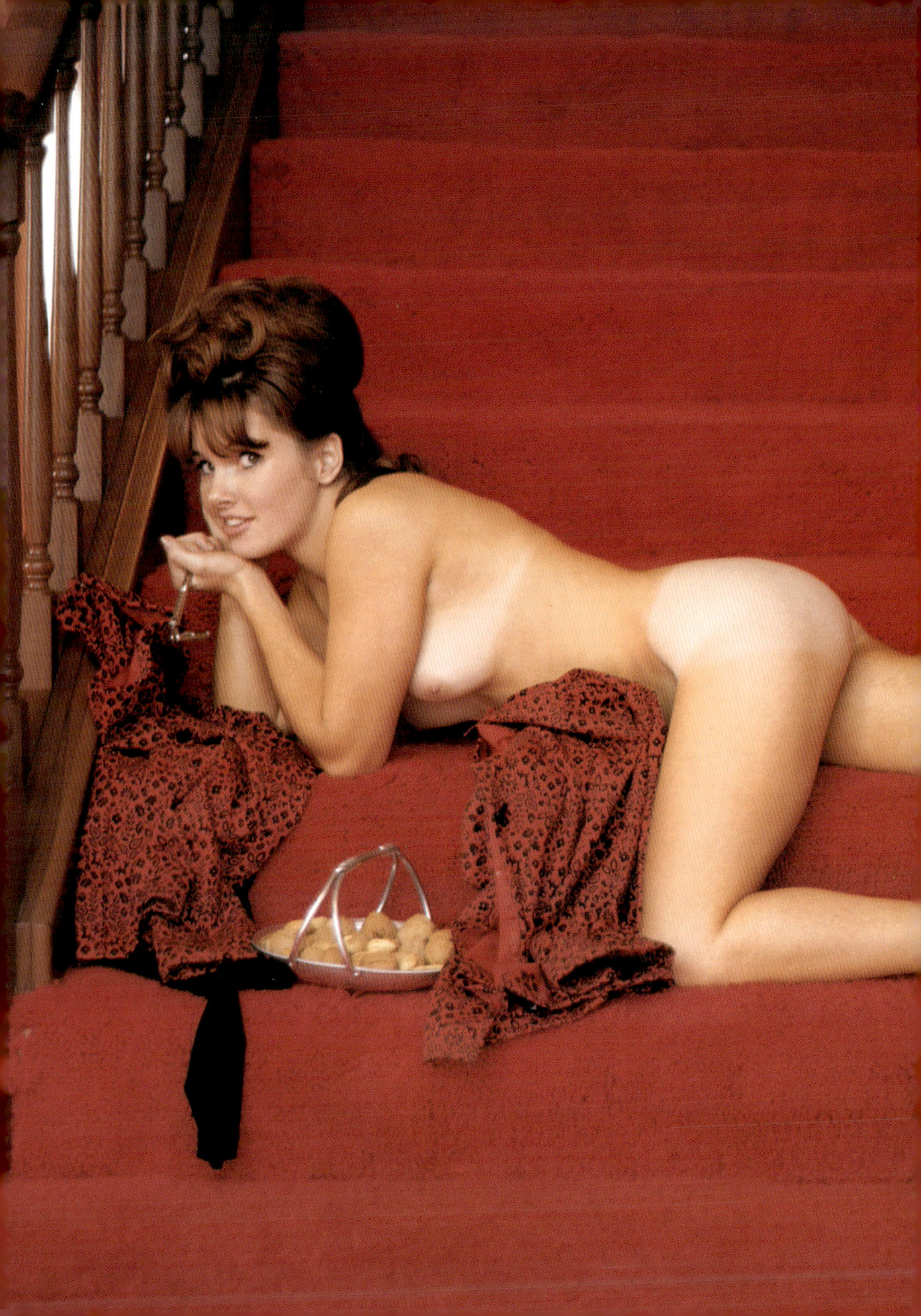

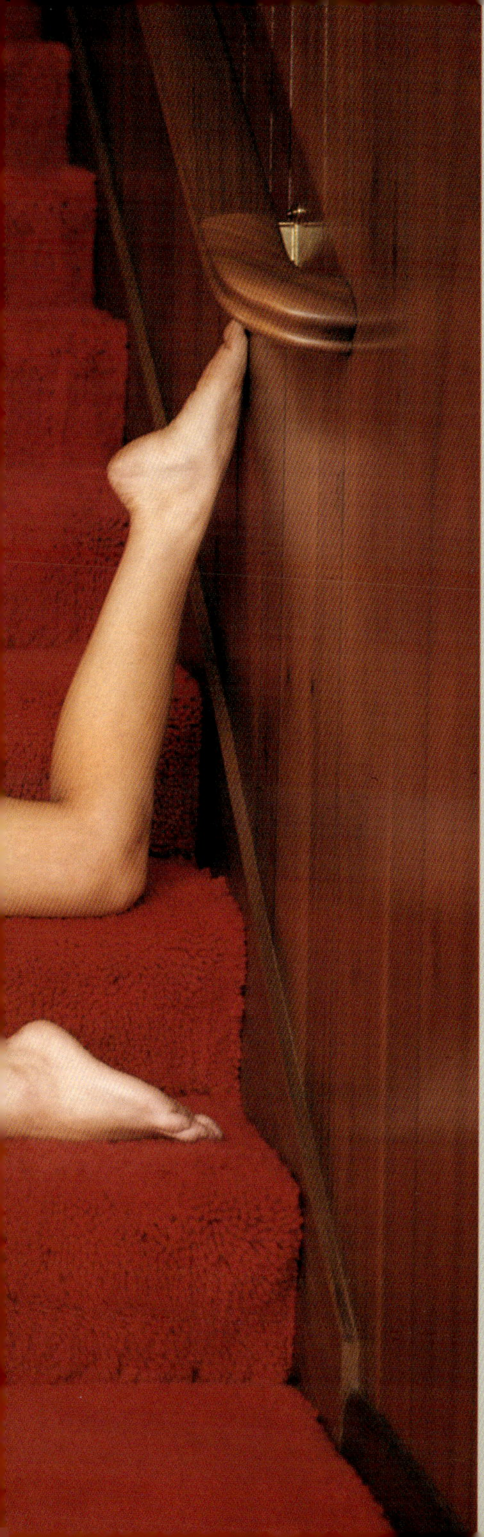

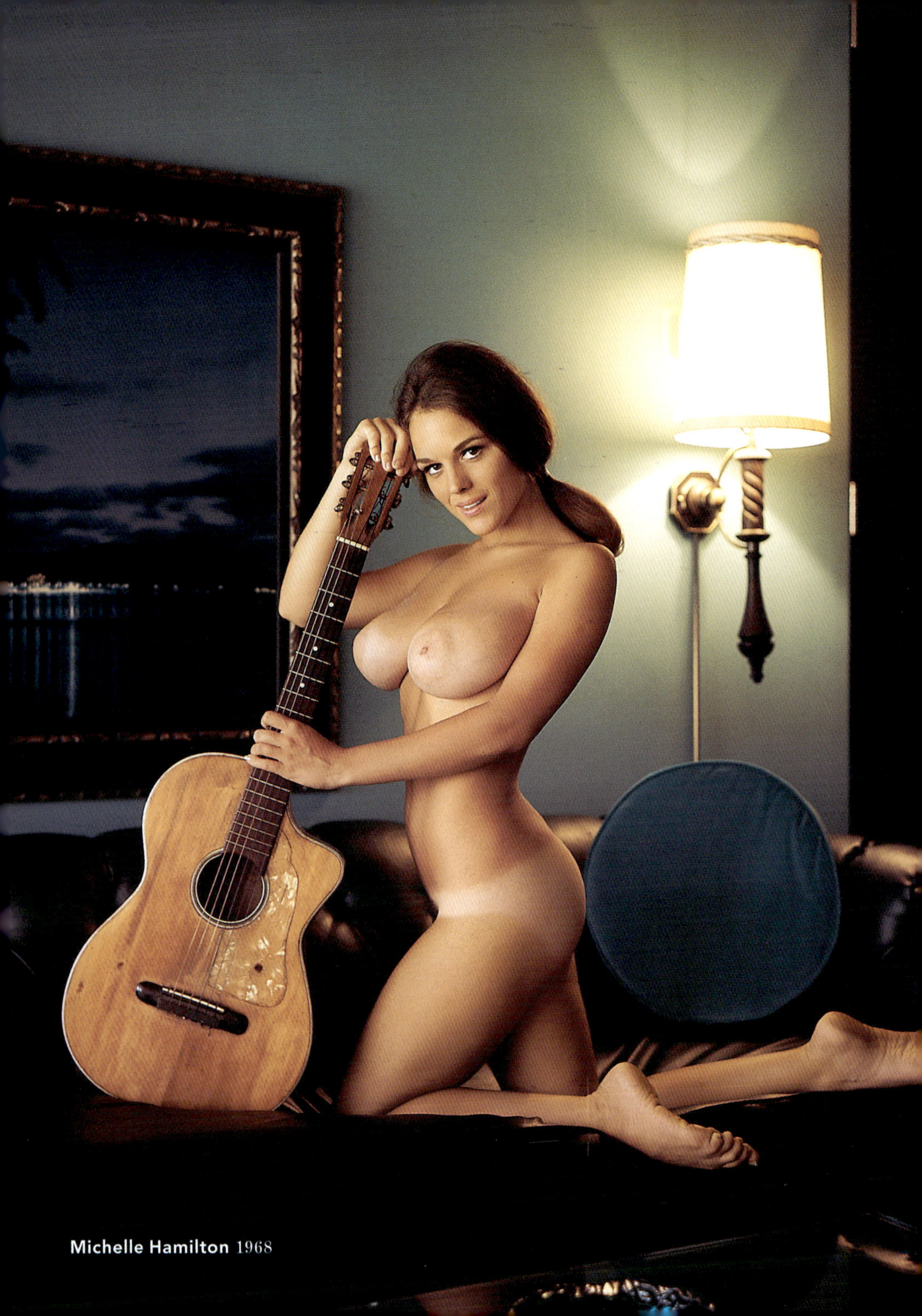

Michelle Hamilton 1968

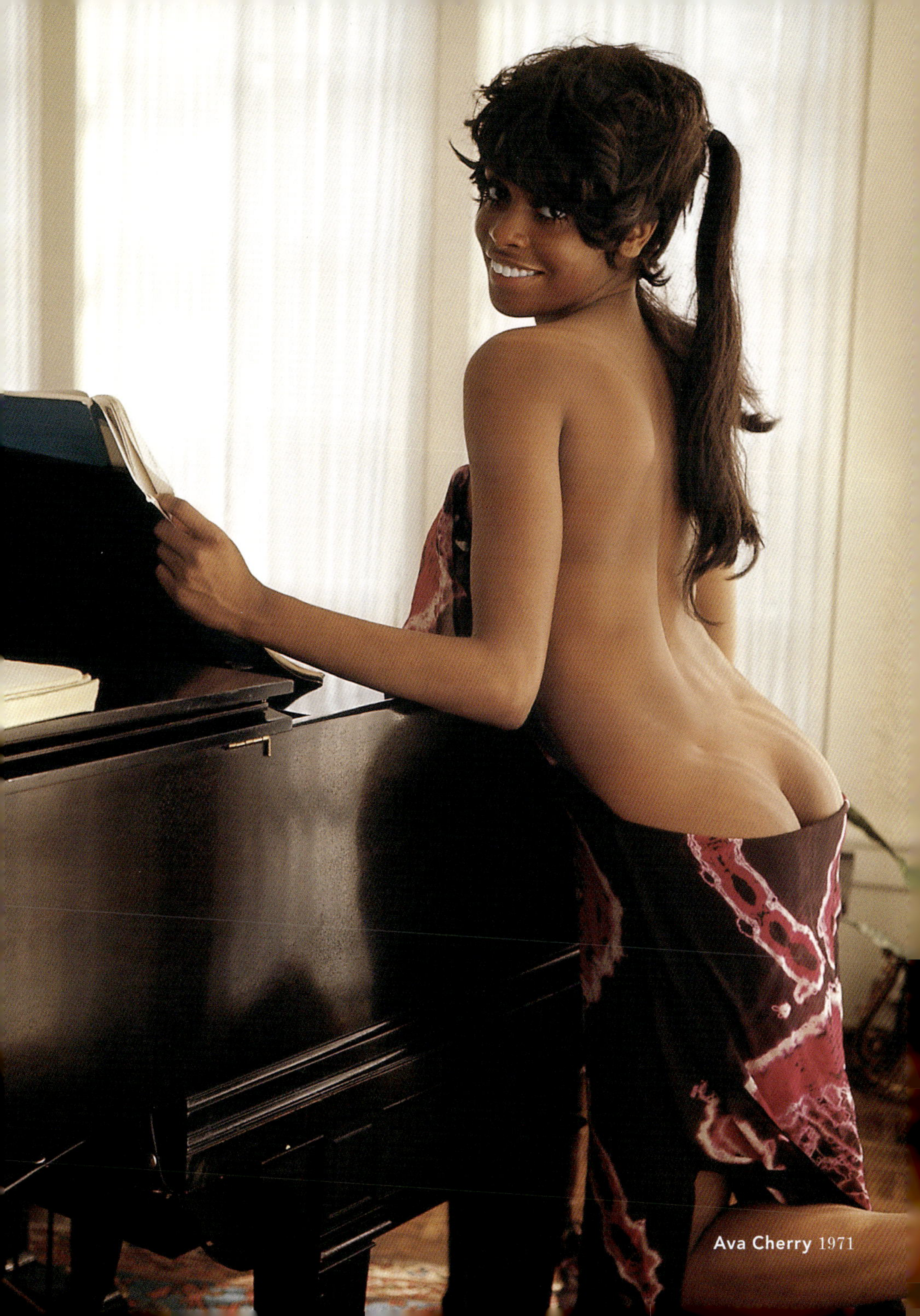

Ava Cherry 1971

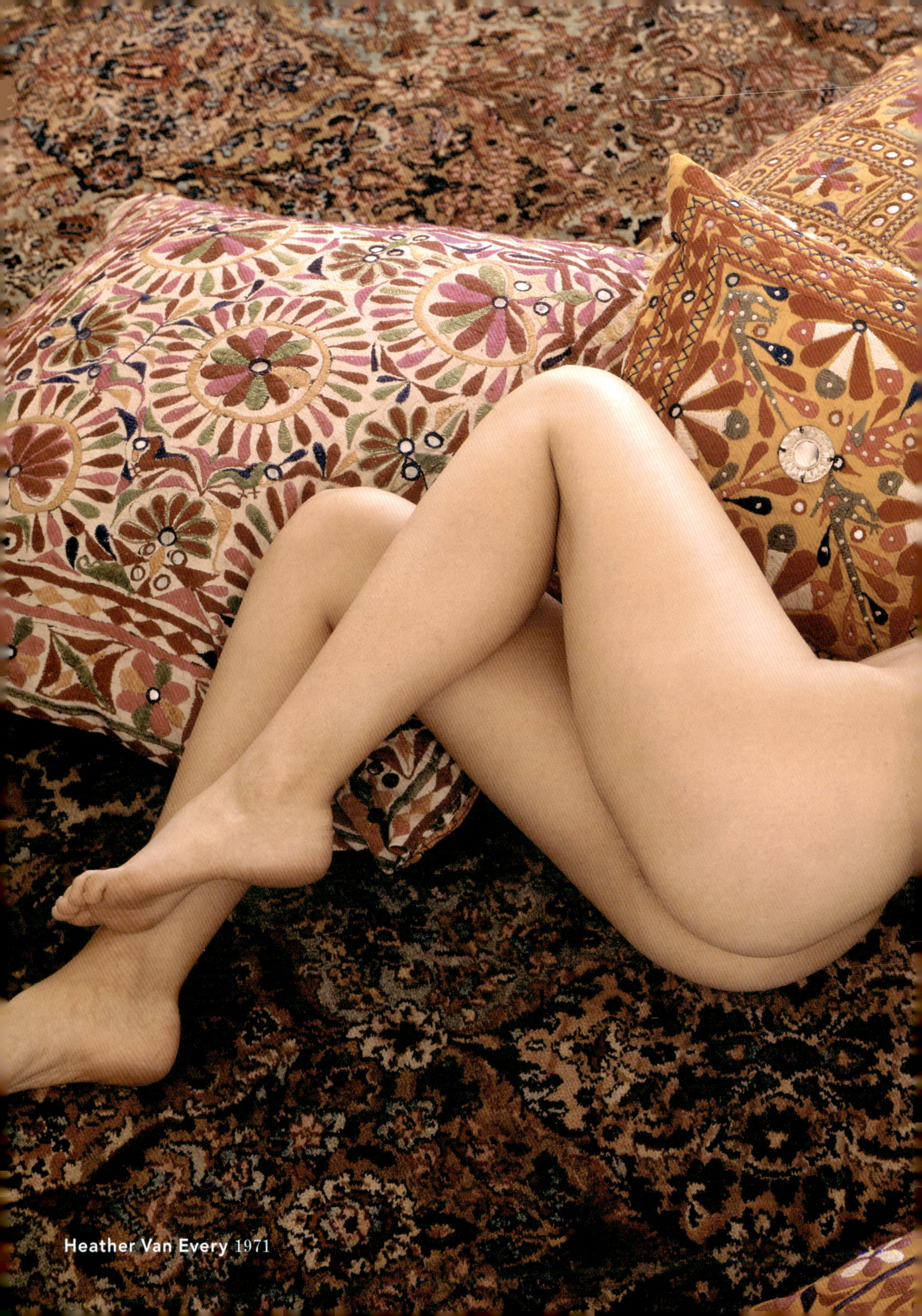

Heather Van Every 1971

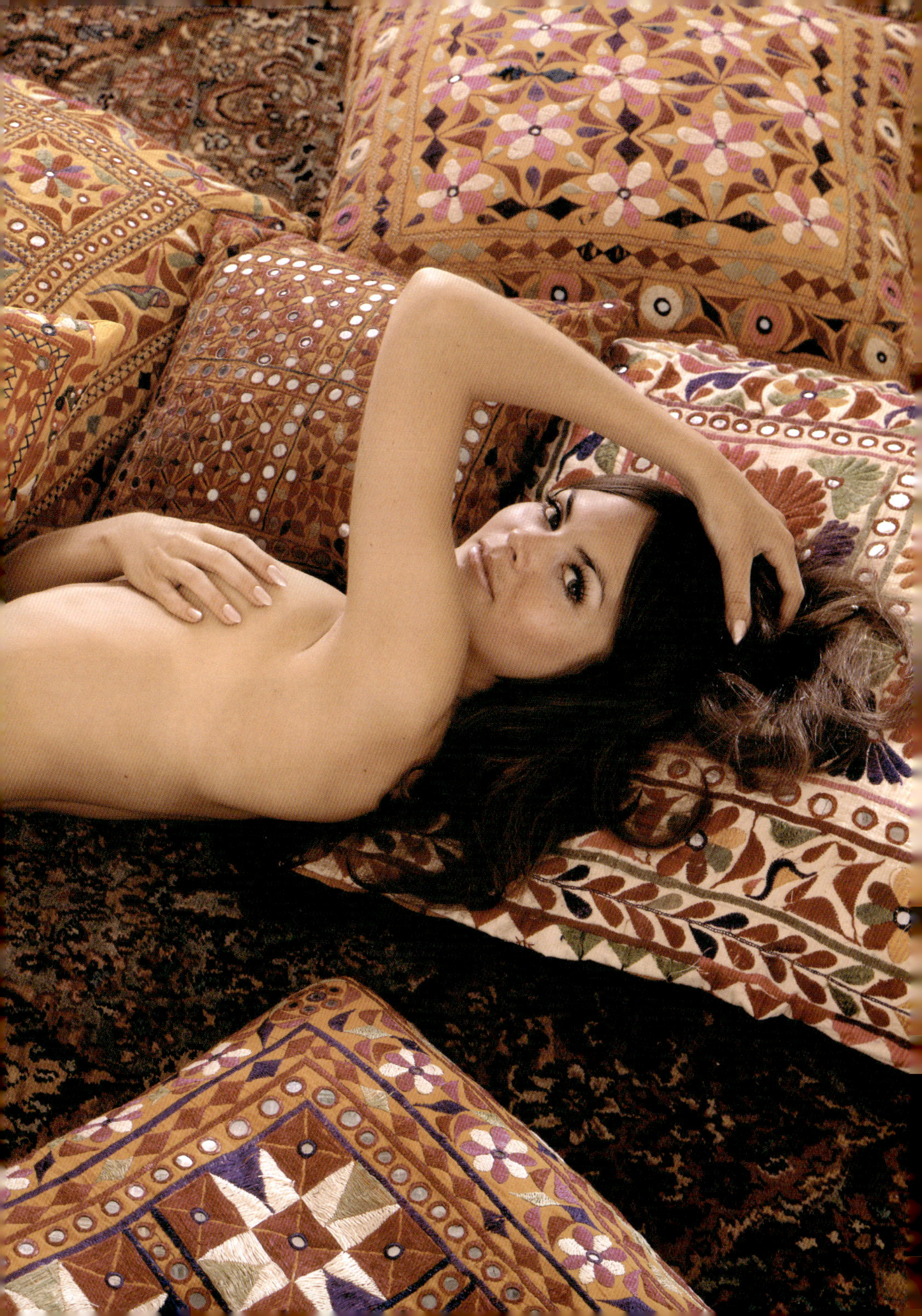

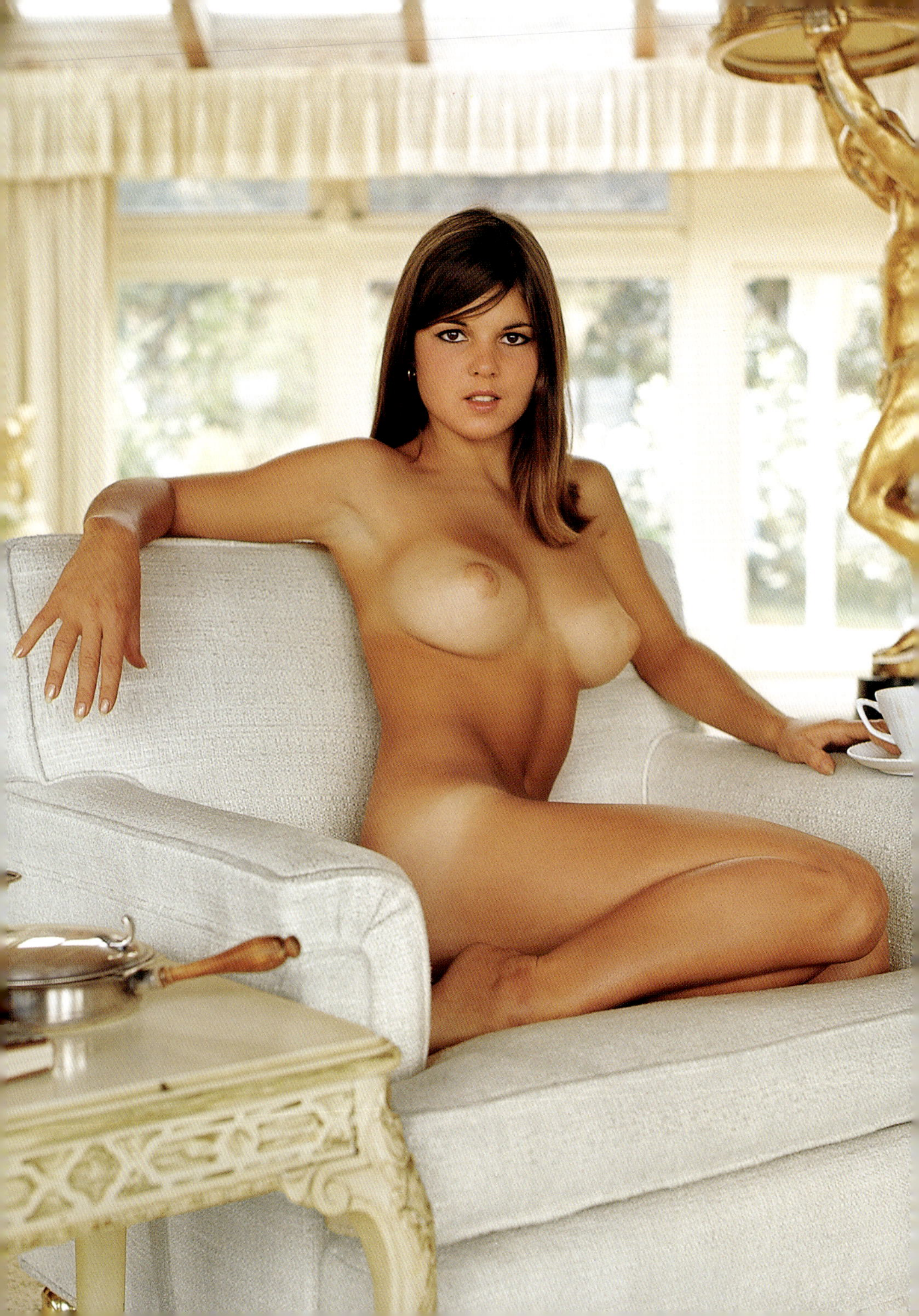

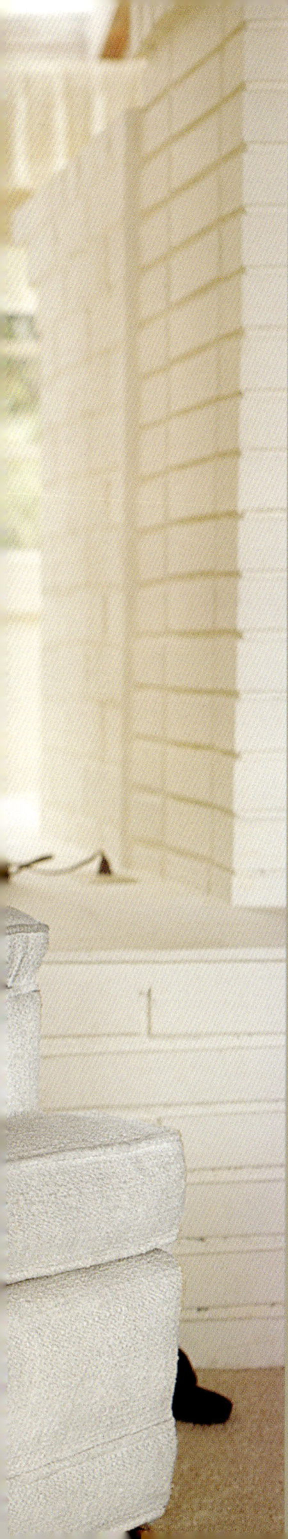

"I think the most important thing a woman can have—next to talent, of course—is her hairdresser."

JOAN CRAWFORD (A BRUNETTE)

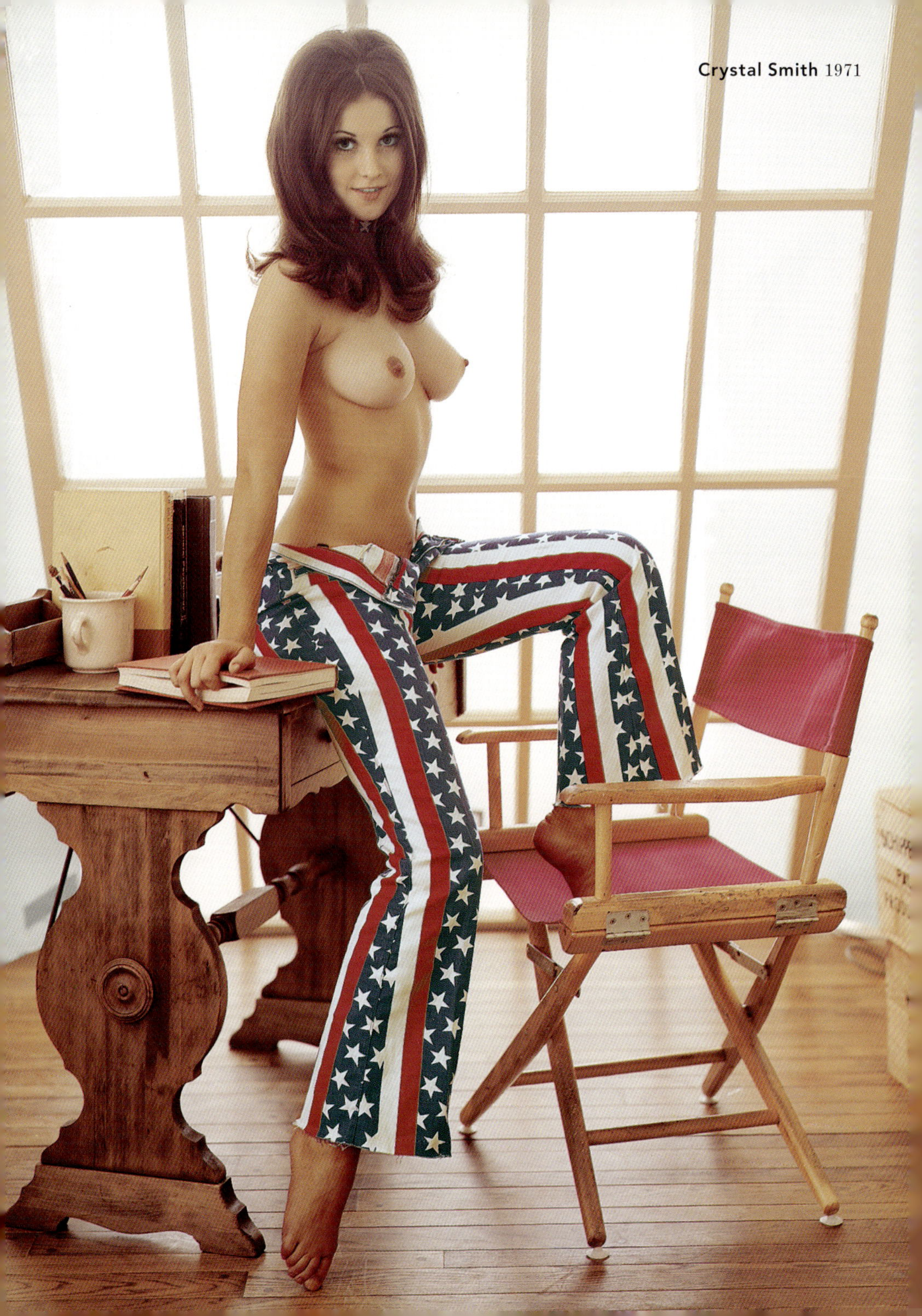

Crystal Smith 1971

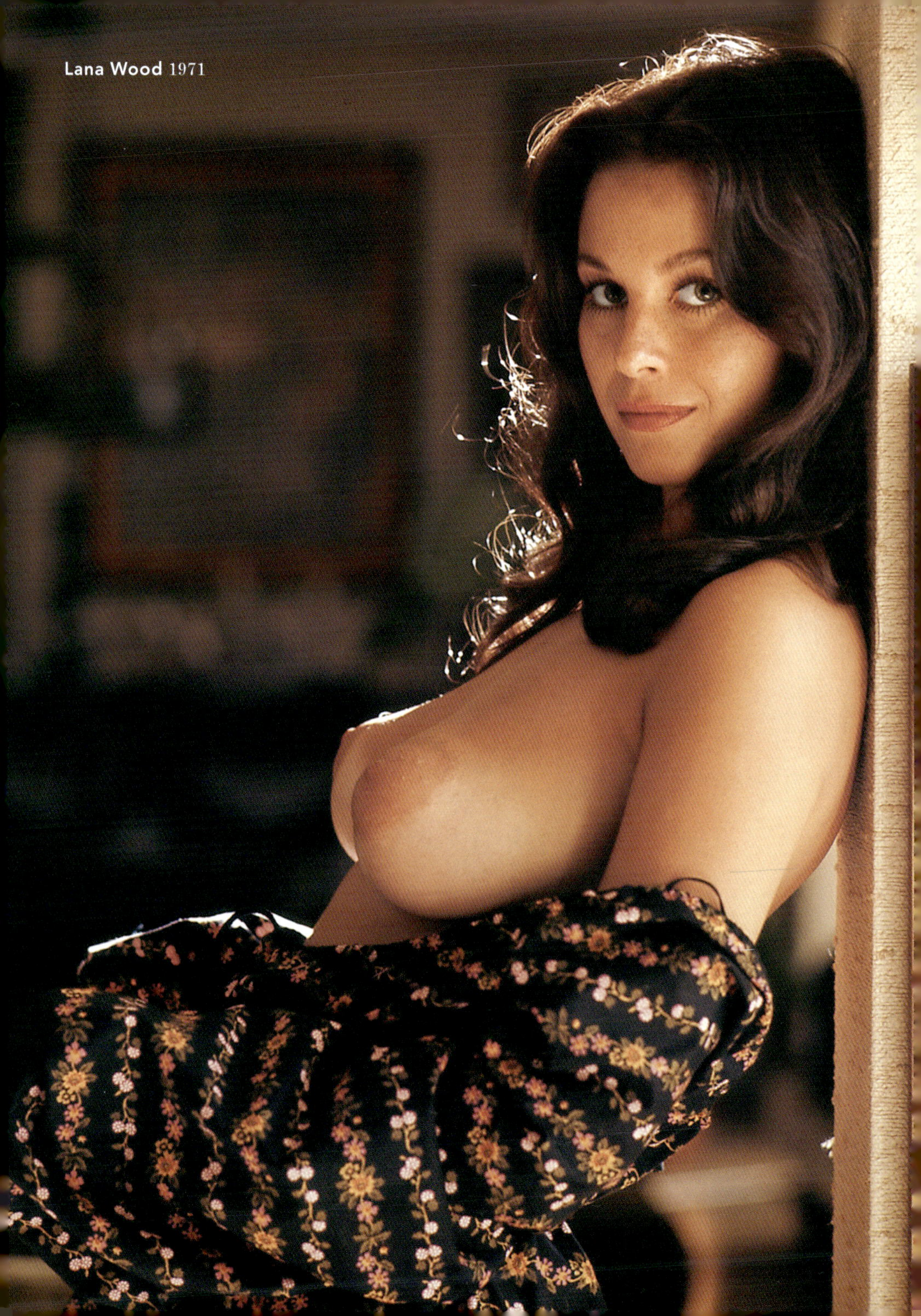

Lana Wood 1971

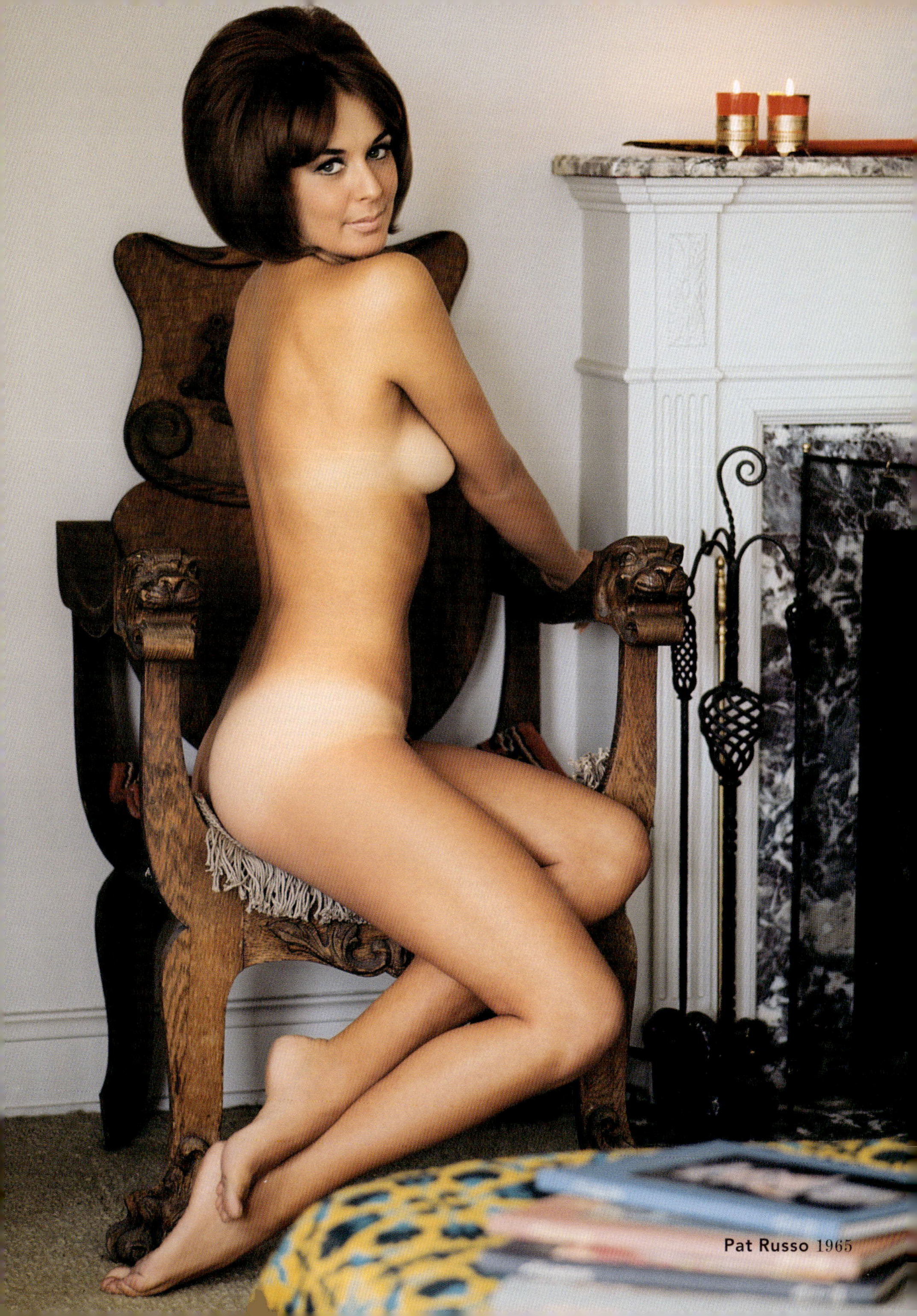

Pat Russo 1965

Sandra Edwards 1957

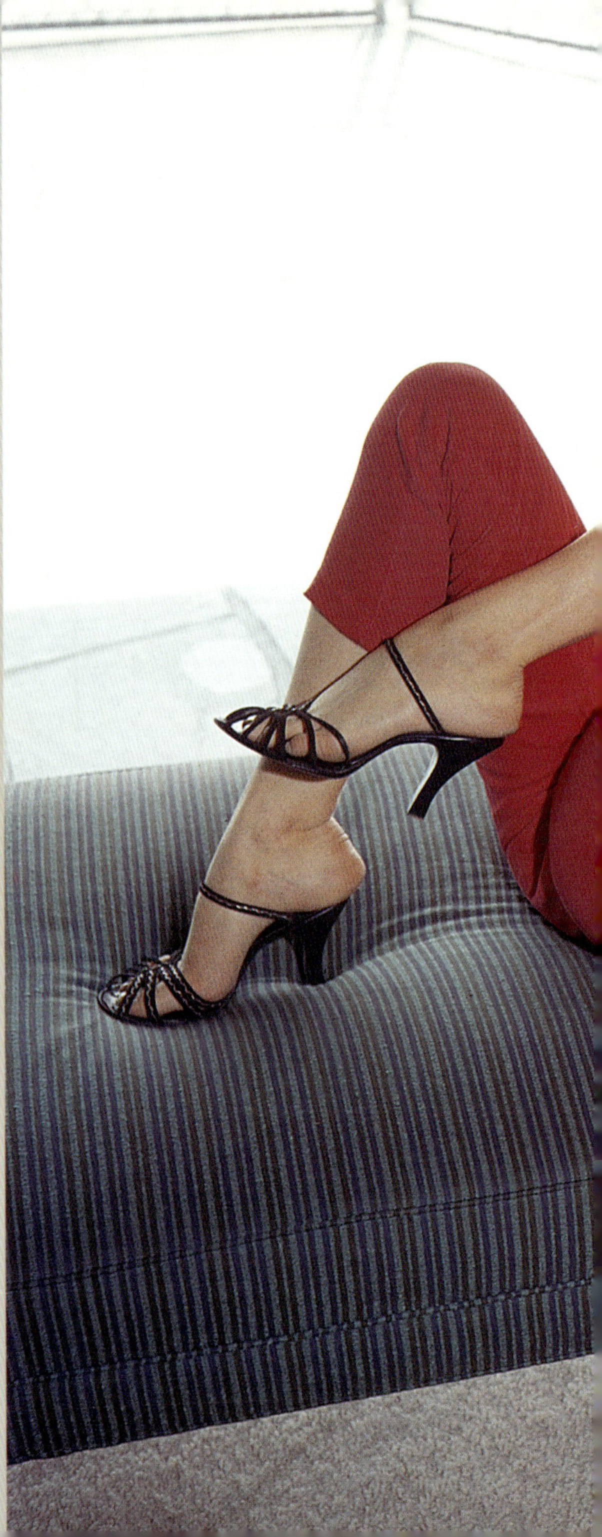

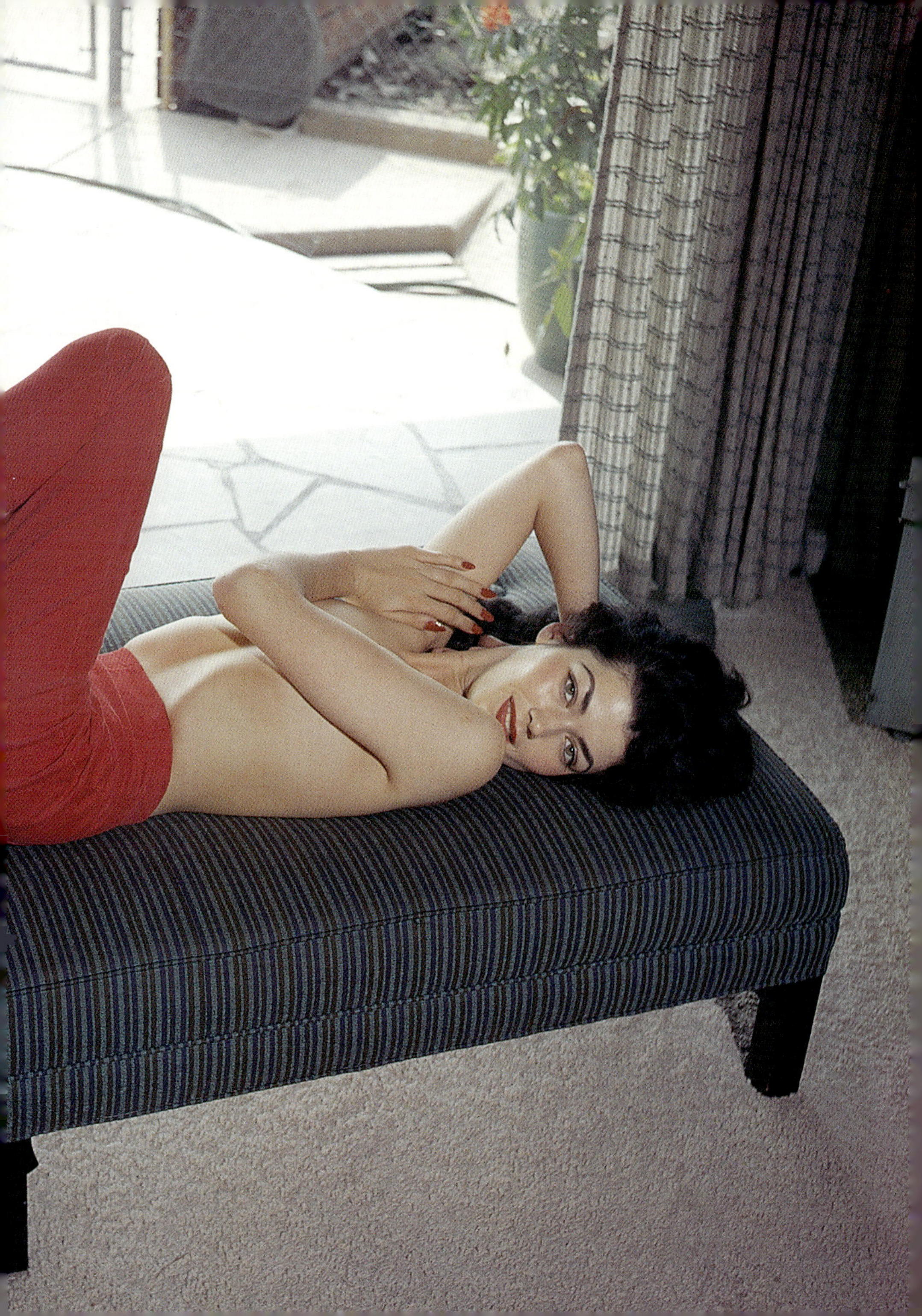

"I want to walk barefoot through your hair."

ROBERT YOUNG TO MYRNA LOY, *NEW MORALS FOR OLD*

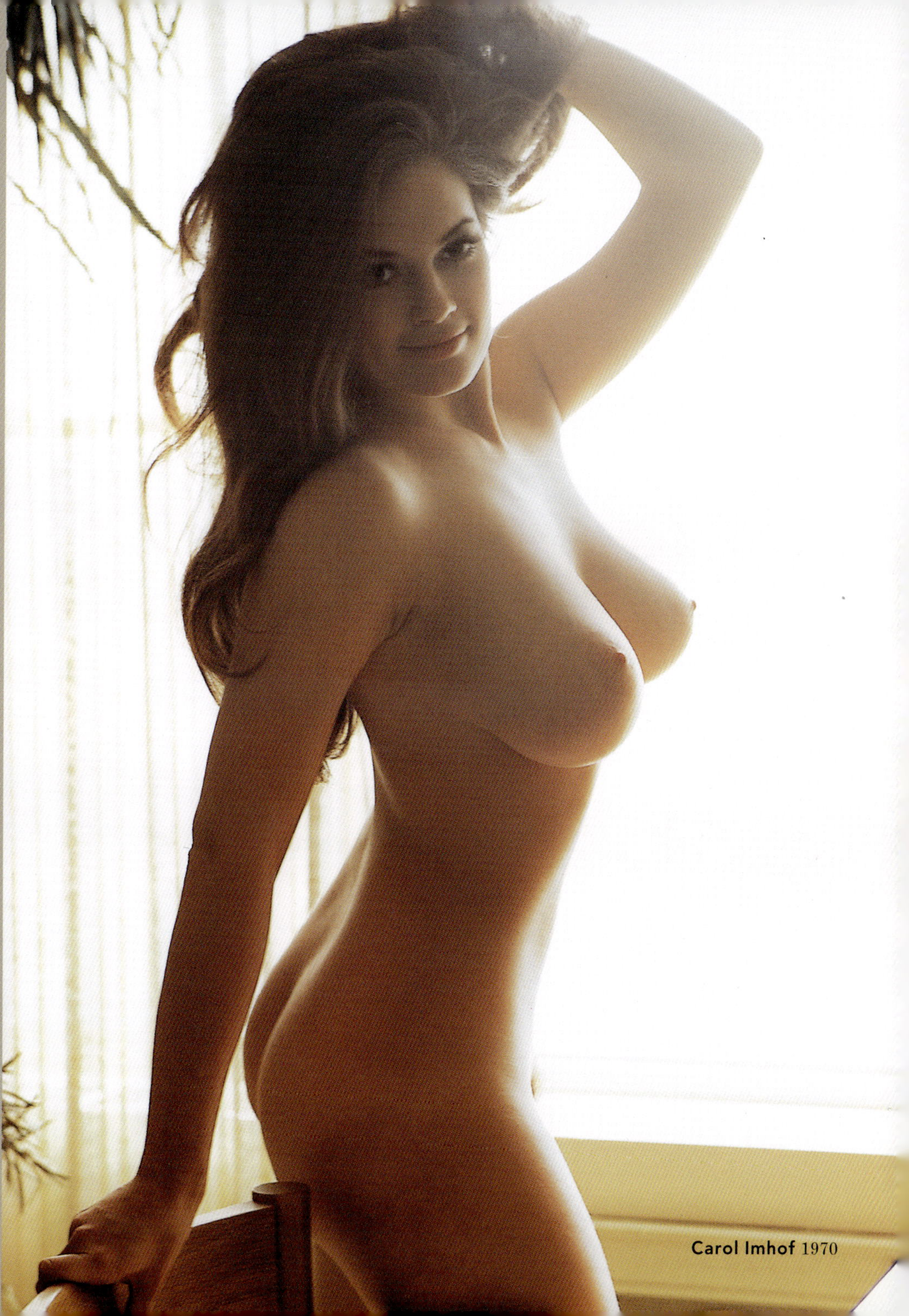

Carol Imhof 1970

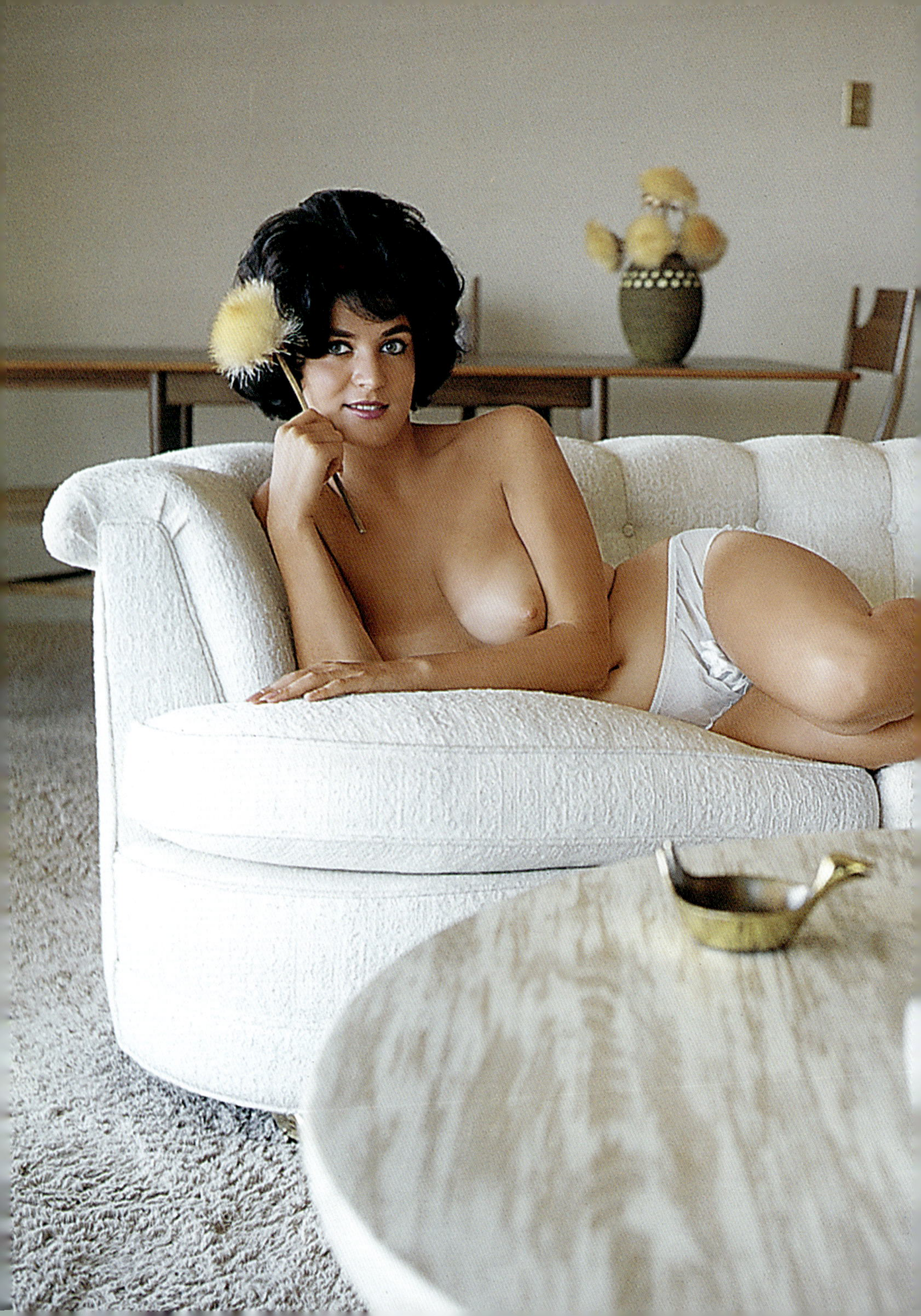

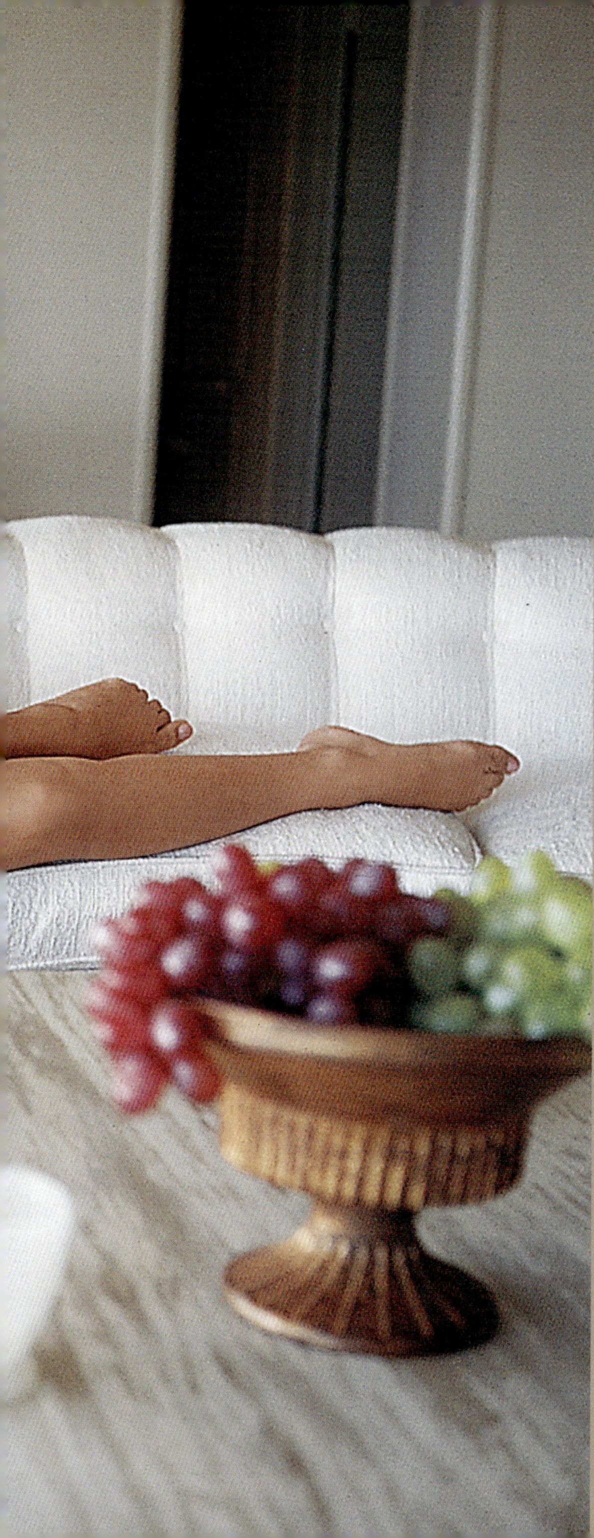

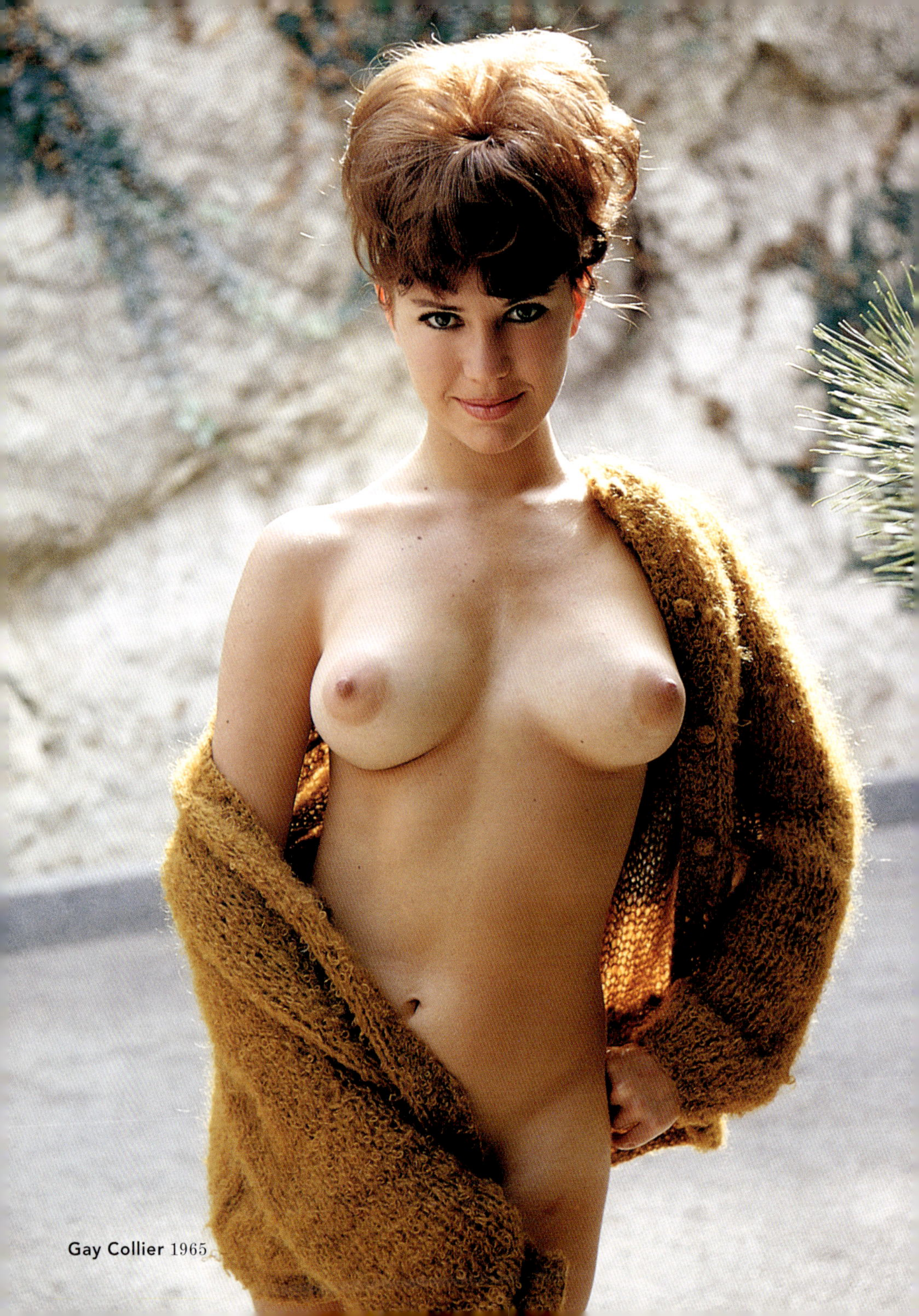

Gay Collier 1965

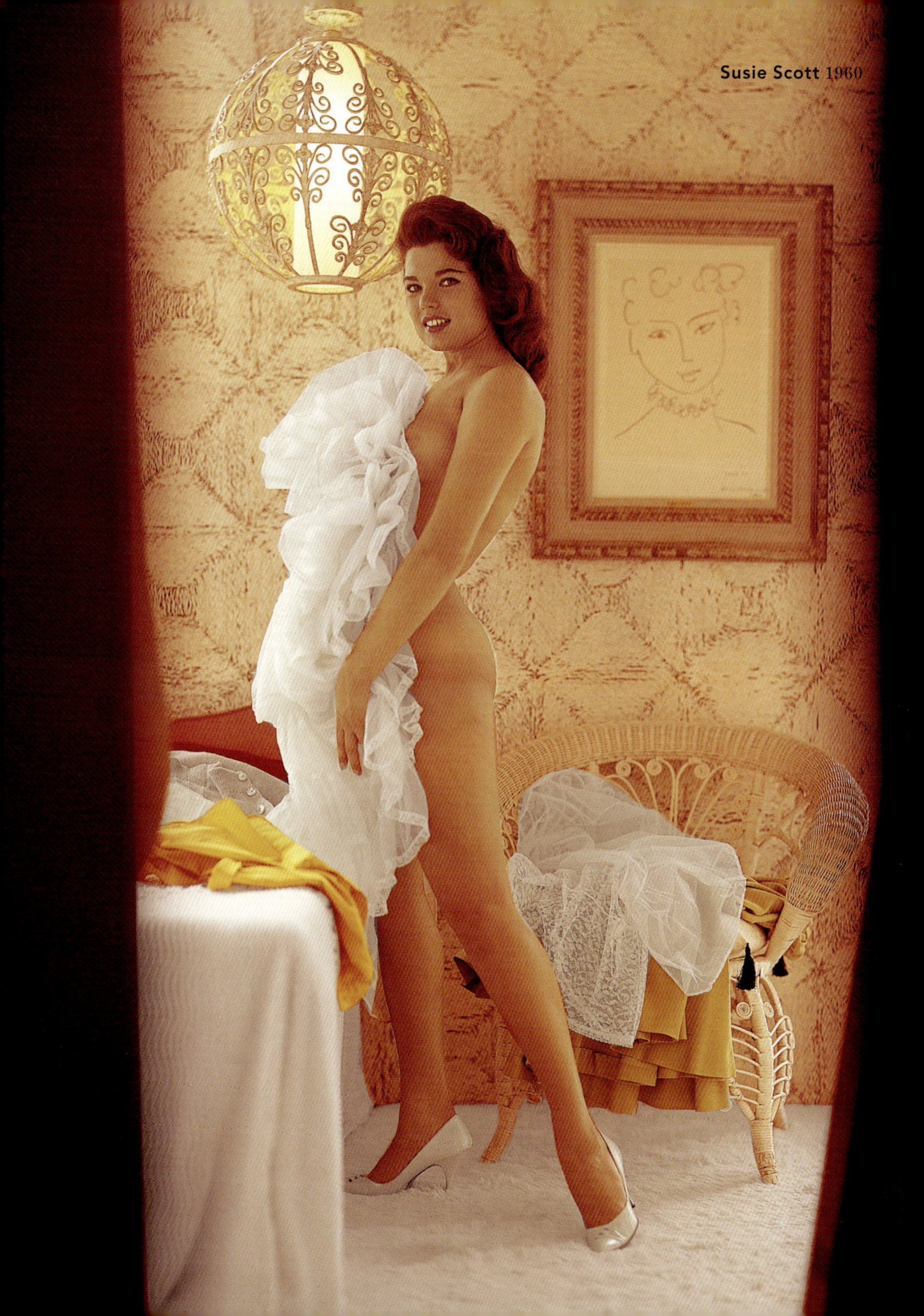

Susie Scott 1960

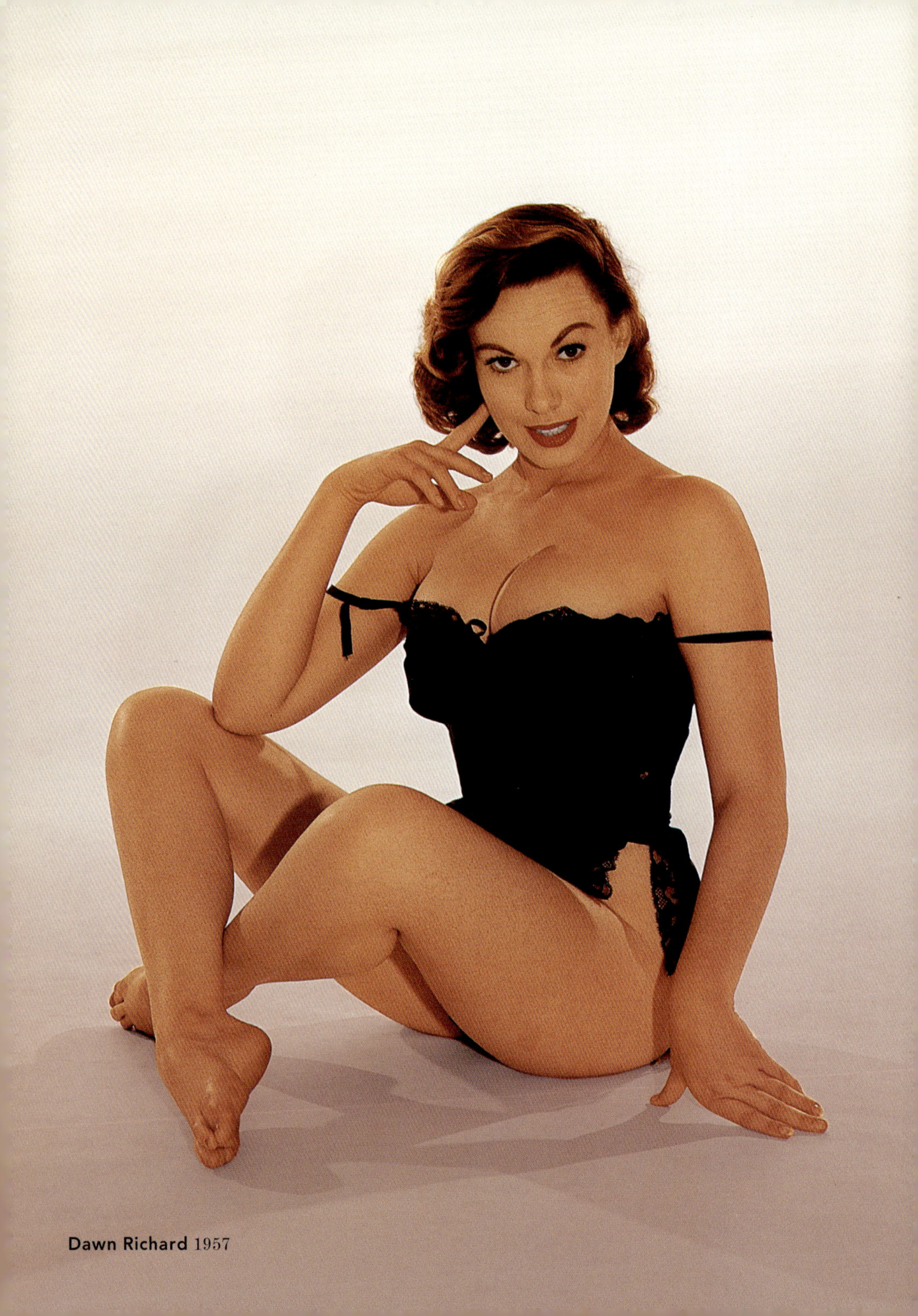

Dawn Richard 1957

"The brunette can make no such stealthy and sure attack. No matter how subtle her art, she can never hope to quite conceal her intent. Her eyes give her away. They flash and glitter. They have depths. They draw the male gaze into mysterious and sinister recesses."

H. L. MENCKEN

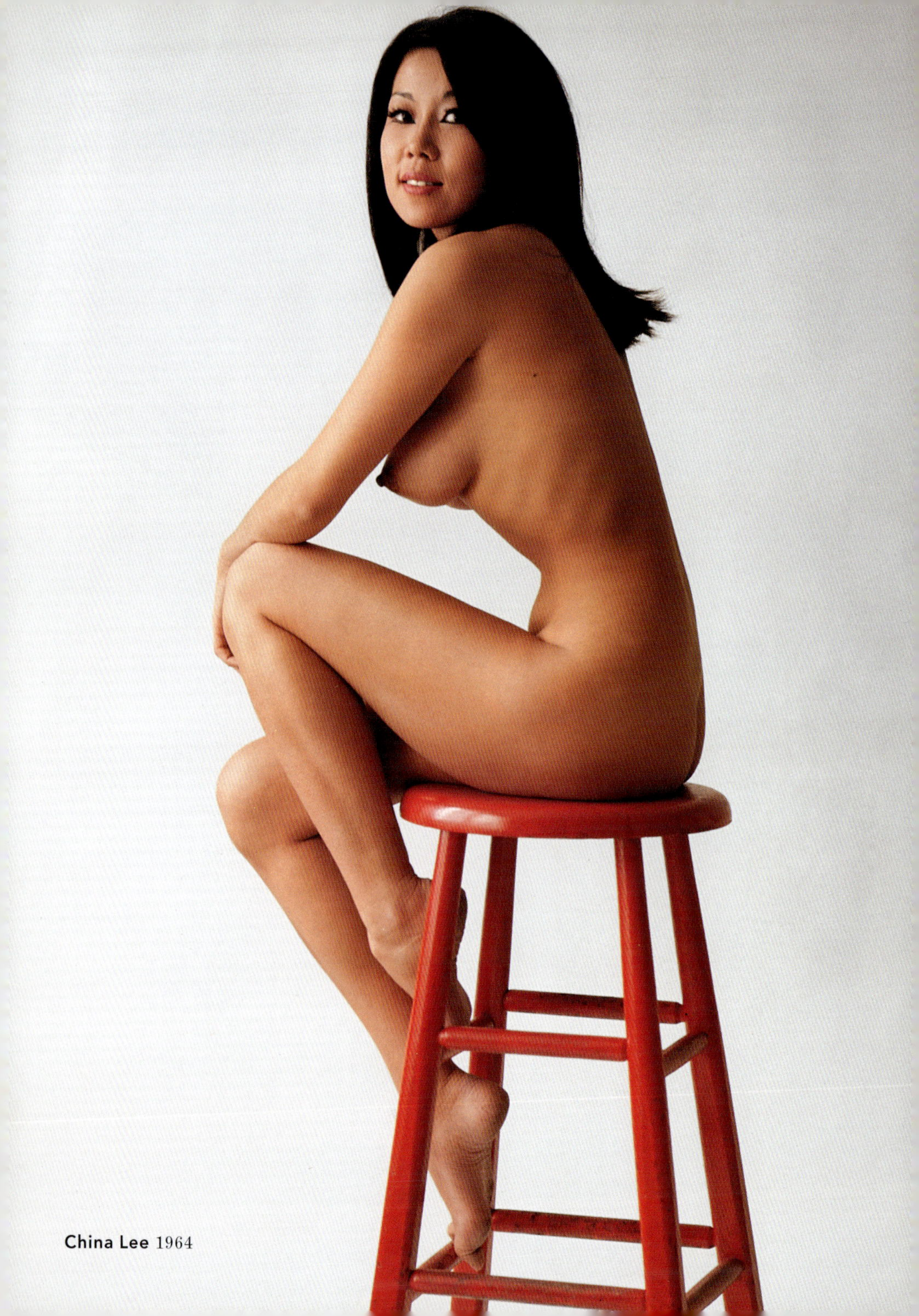

China Lee 1964

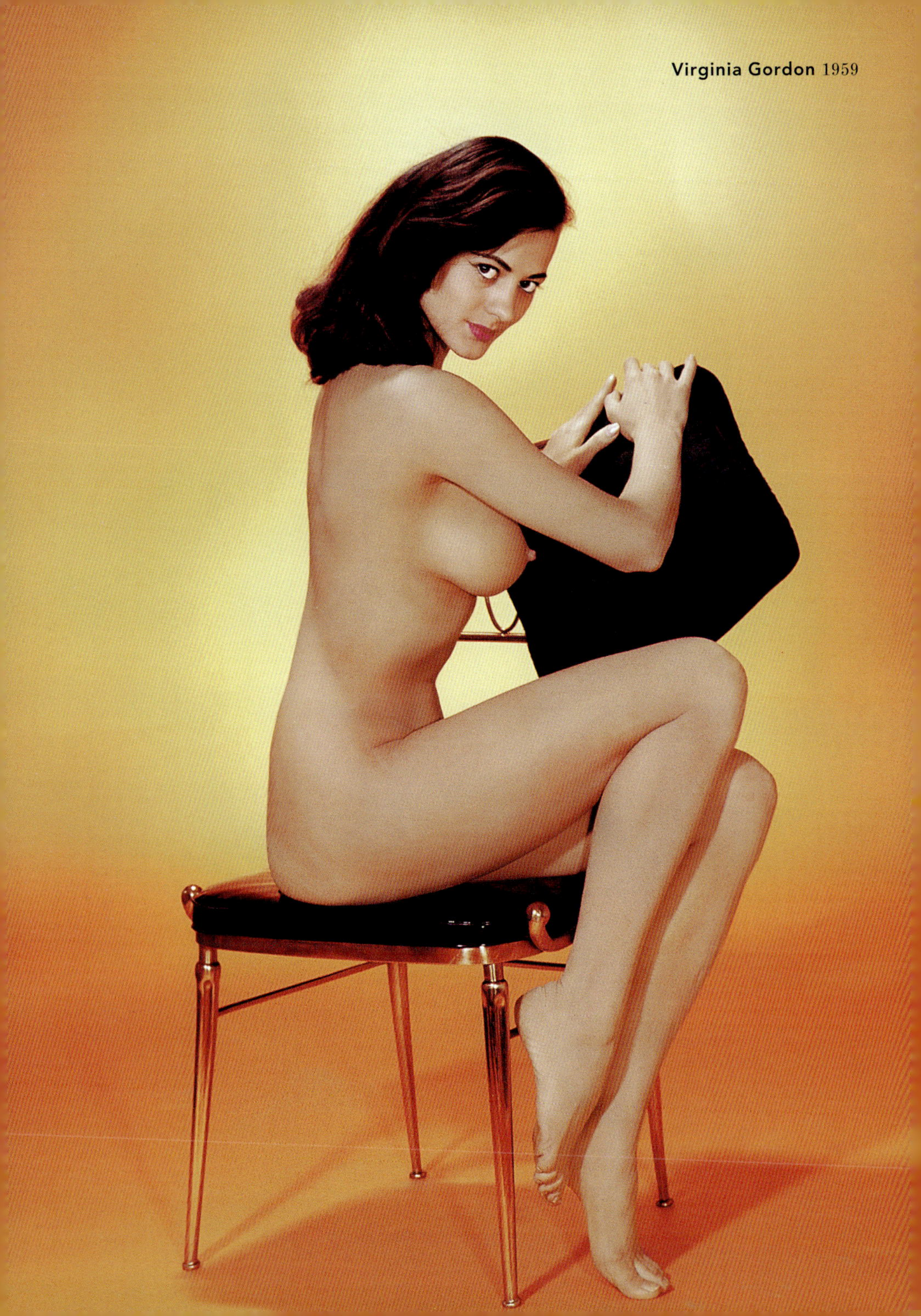

Virginia Gordon 1959

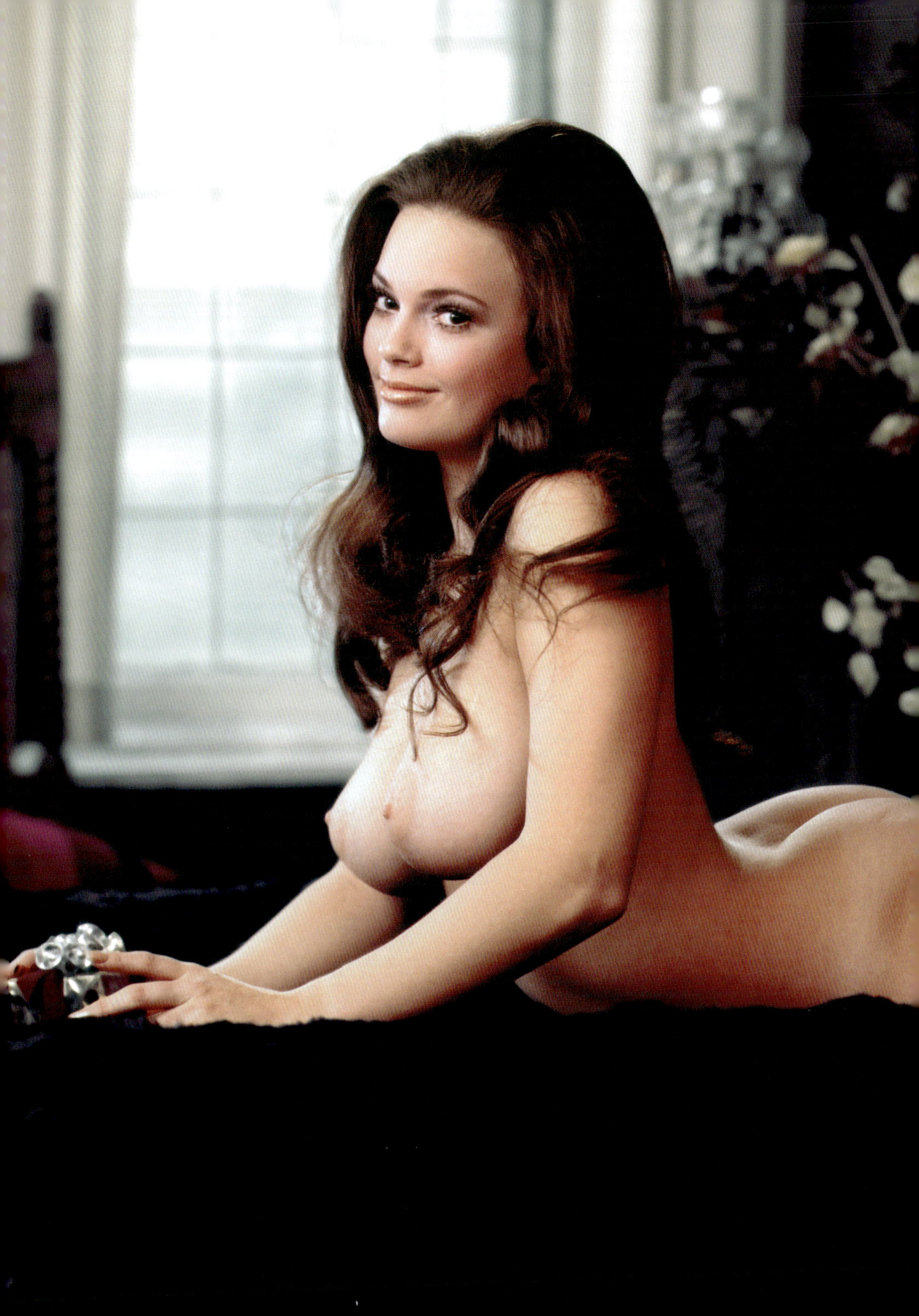

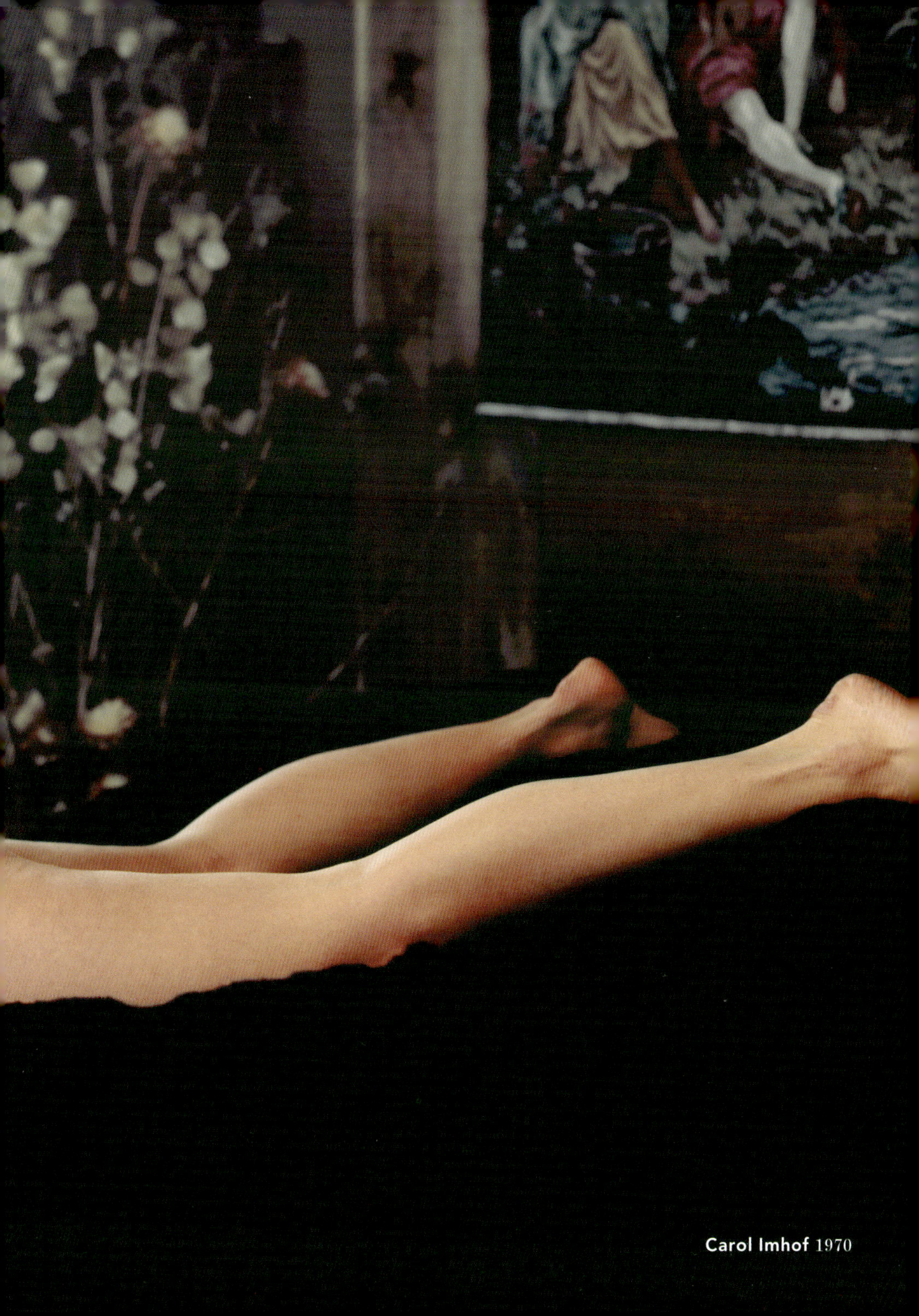

Carol Imhof 1970

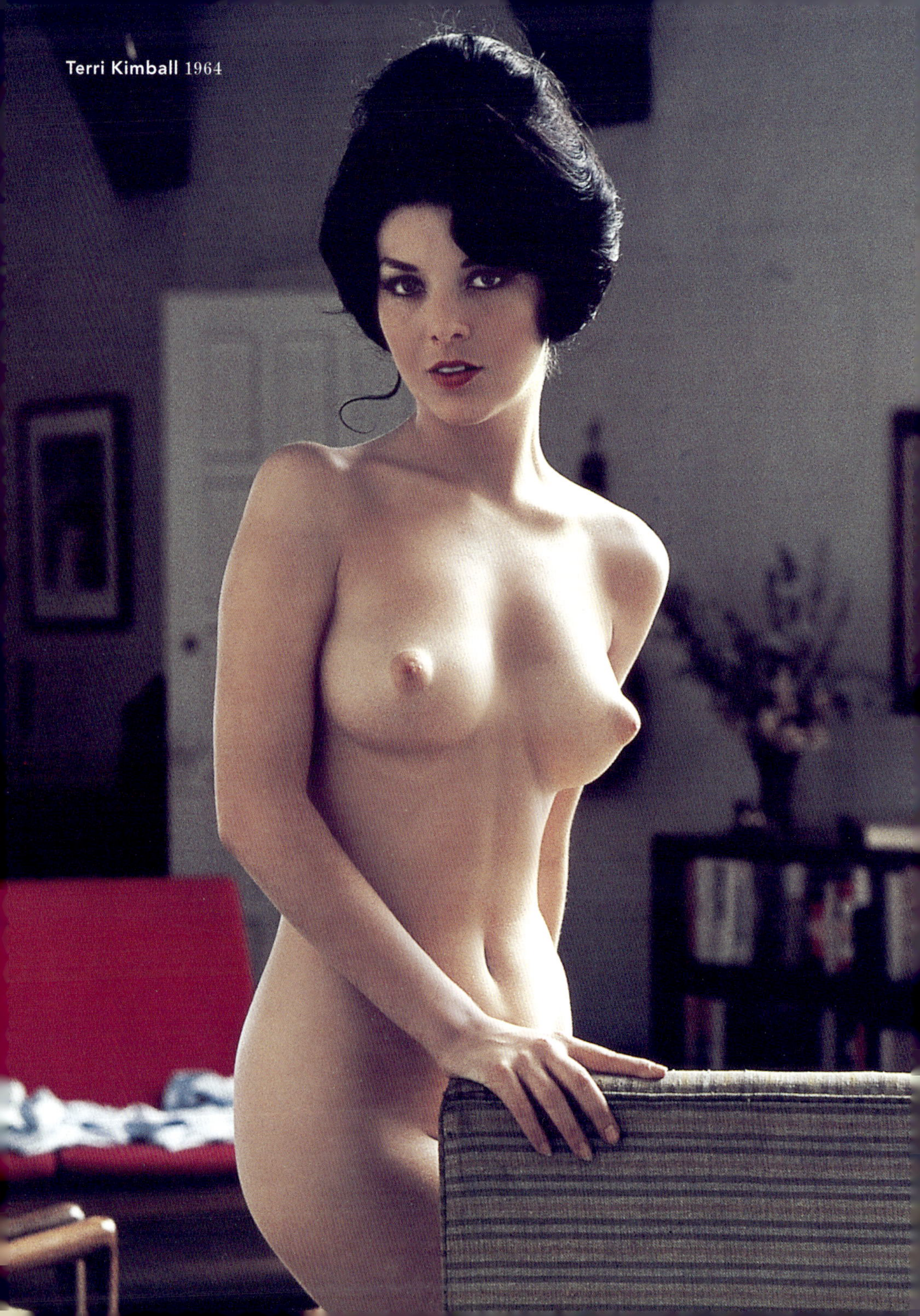

Terri Kimball 1964

"Hair like black ice cream."

ROBERT HUGHES

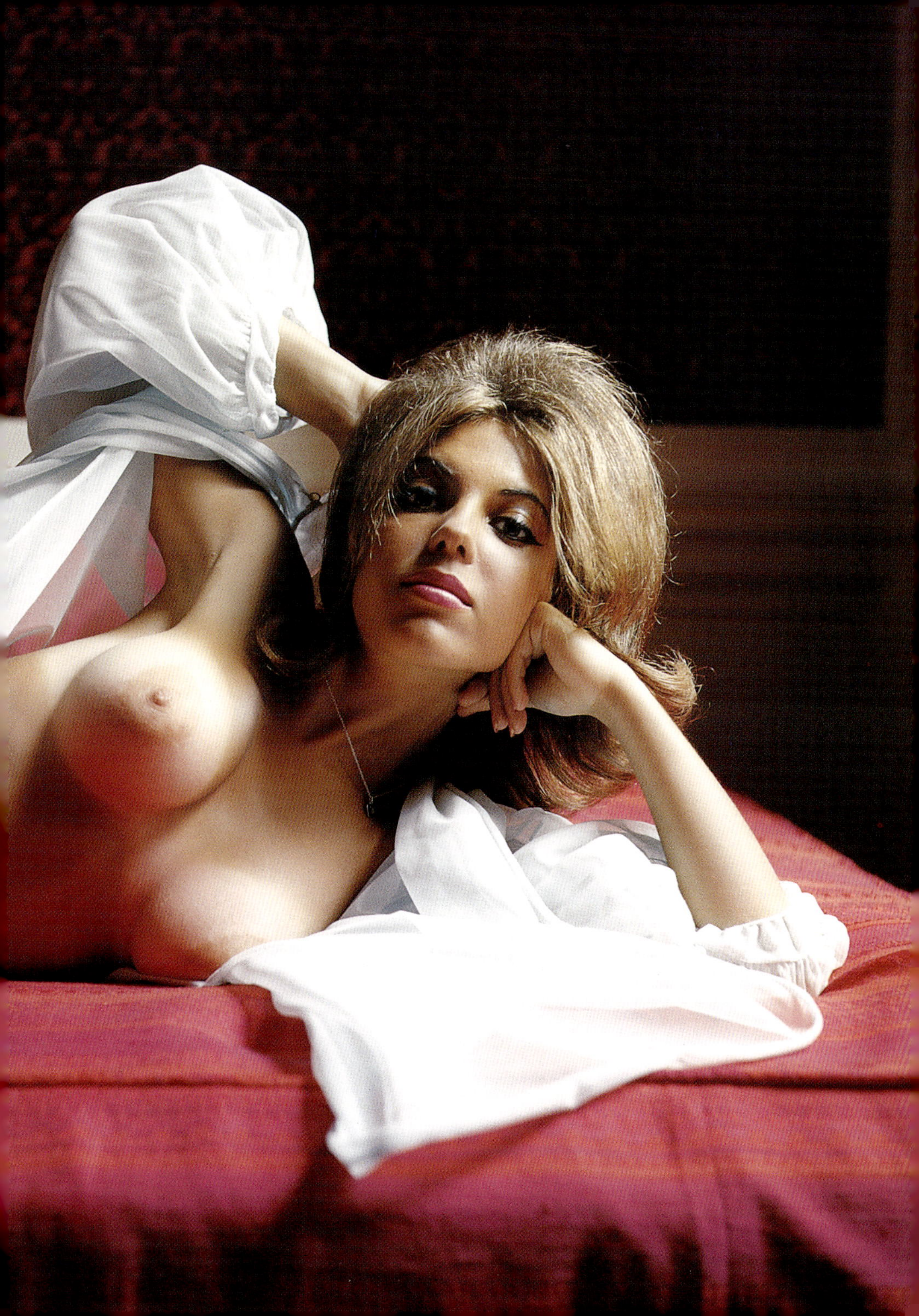

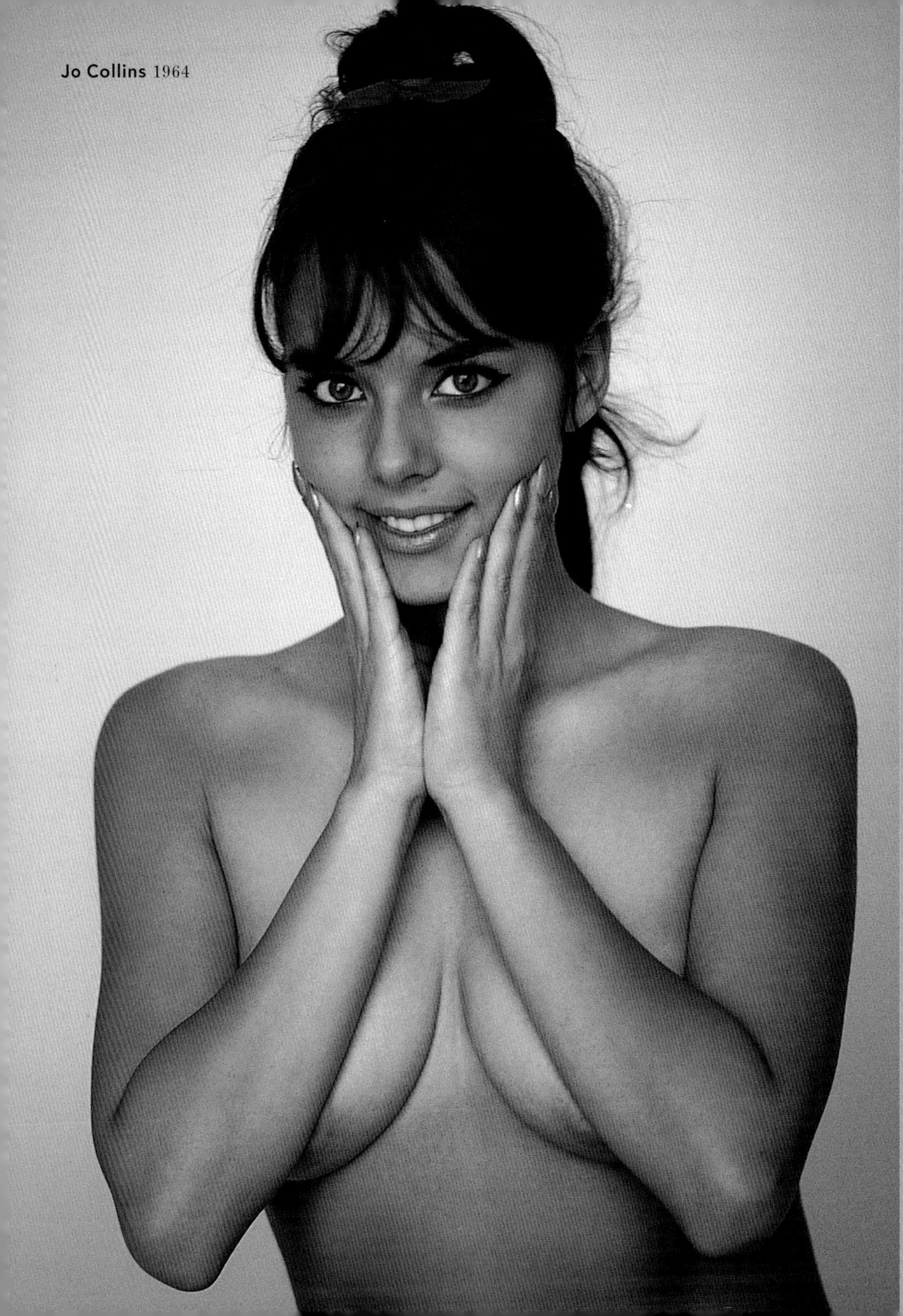

Jo Collins 1964

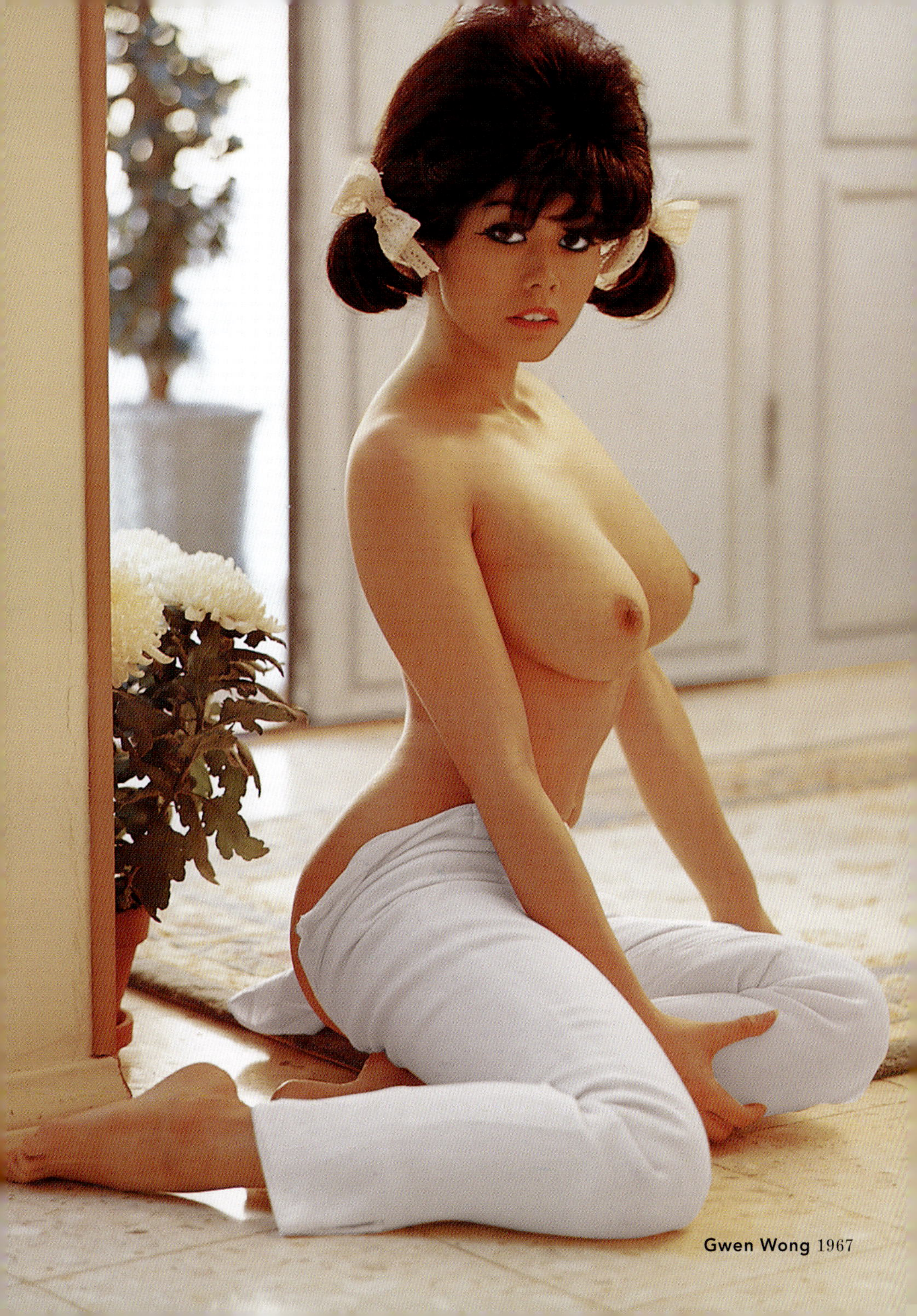

Gwen Wong 1967

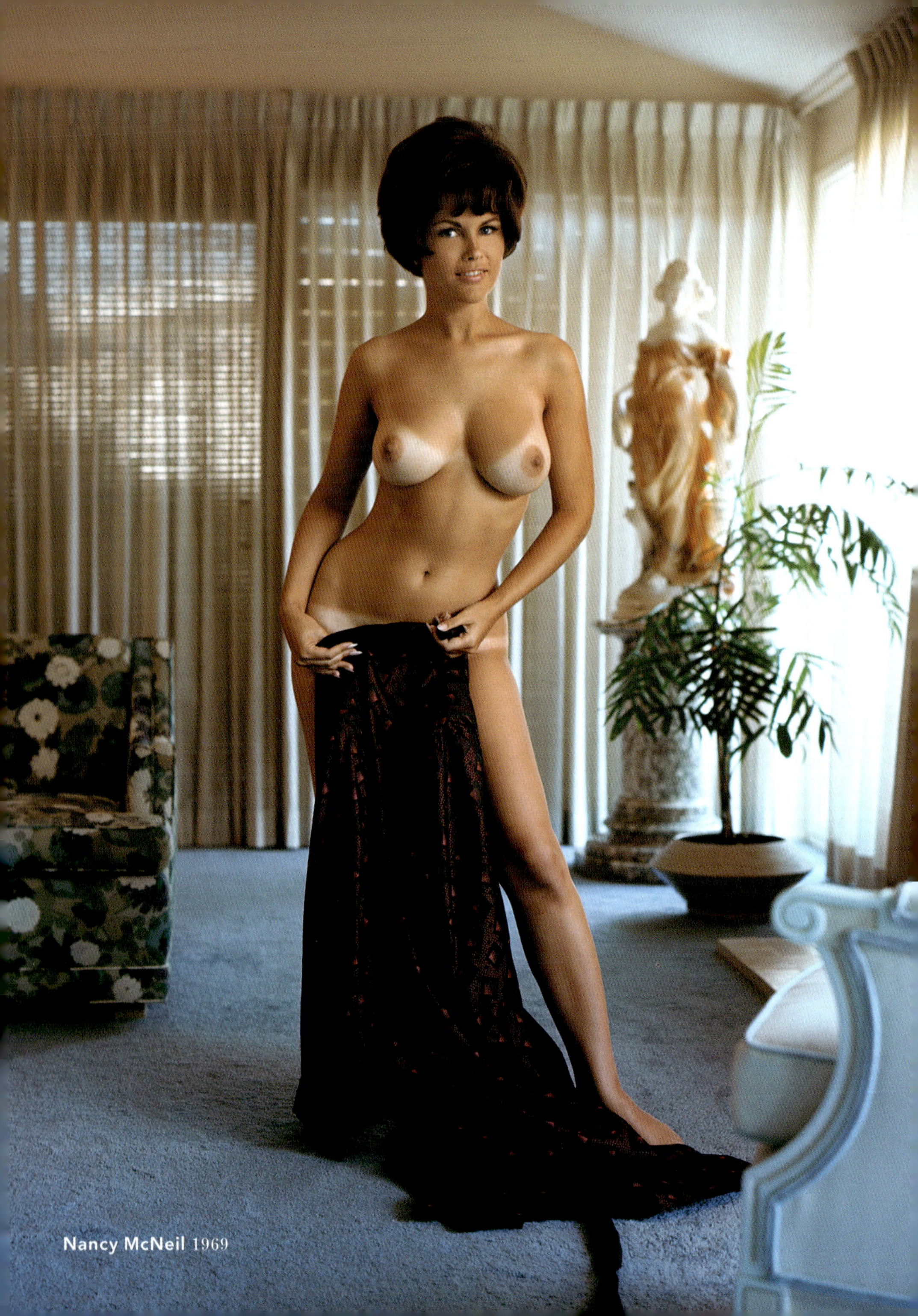

Nancy McNeil 1969

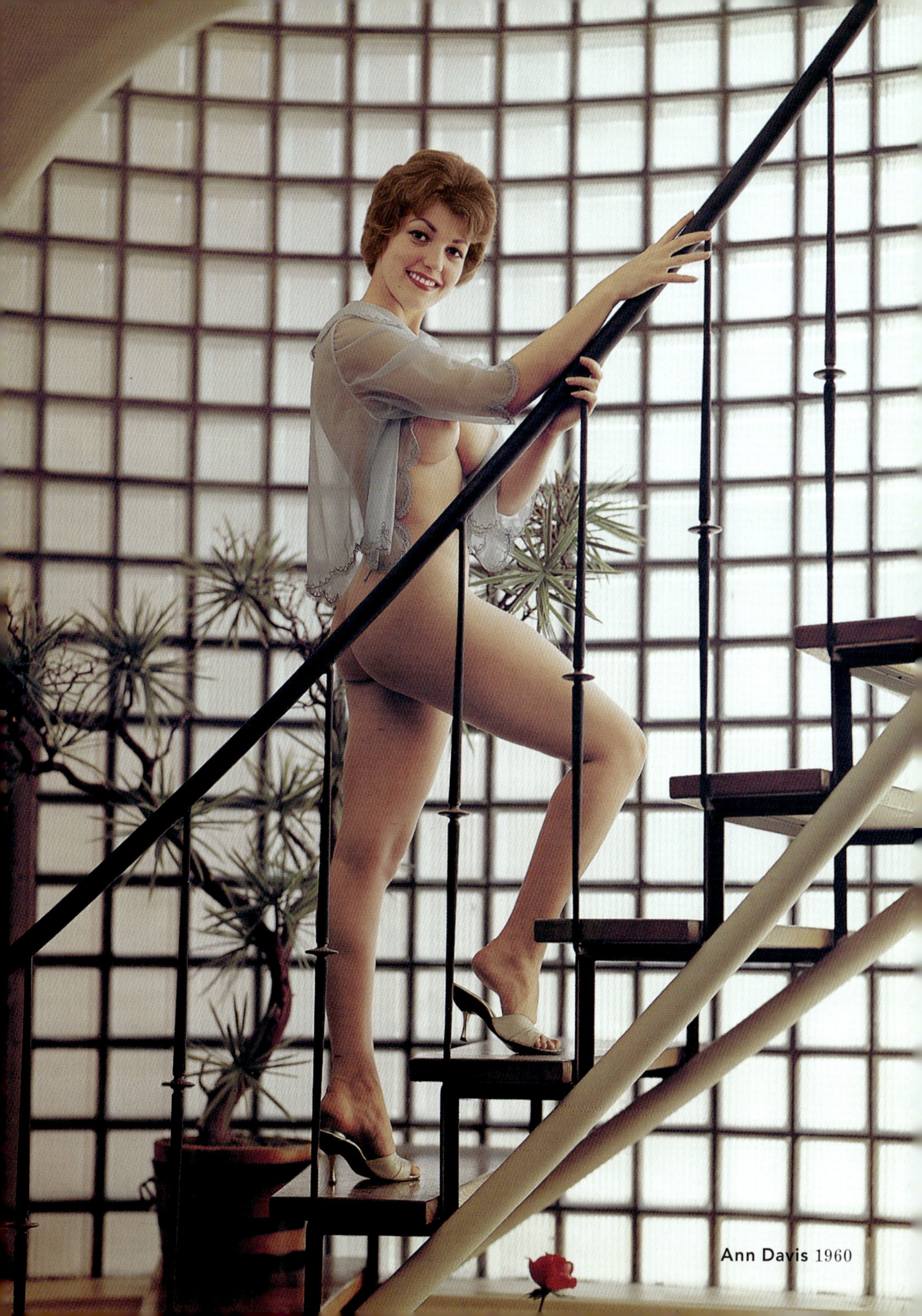

Ann Davis 1960

"The vamp—the predatory and dangerous woman who challenges the male desire for sexual domination—is almost always dark-haired."

WENDY COOPER, *HAIR: SEX, SOCIETY, SYMBOLISM*

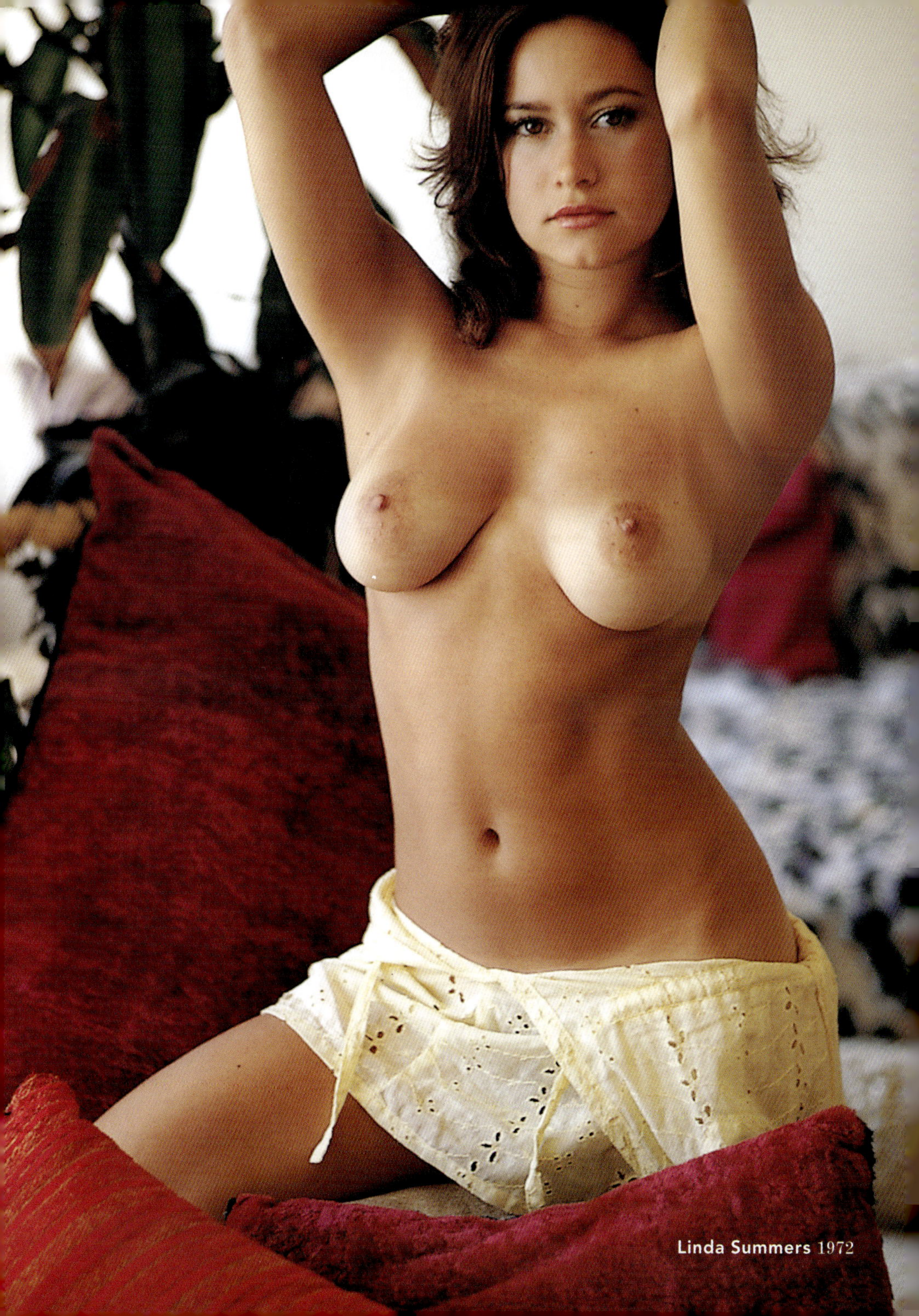

Linda Summers 1972

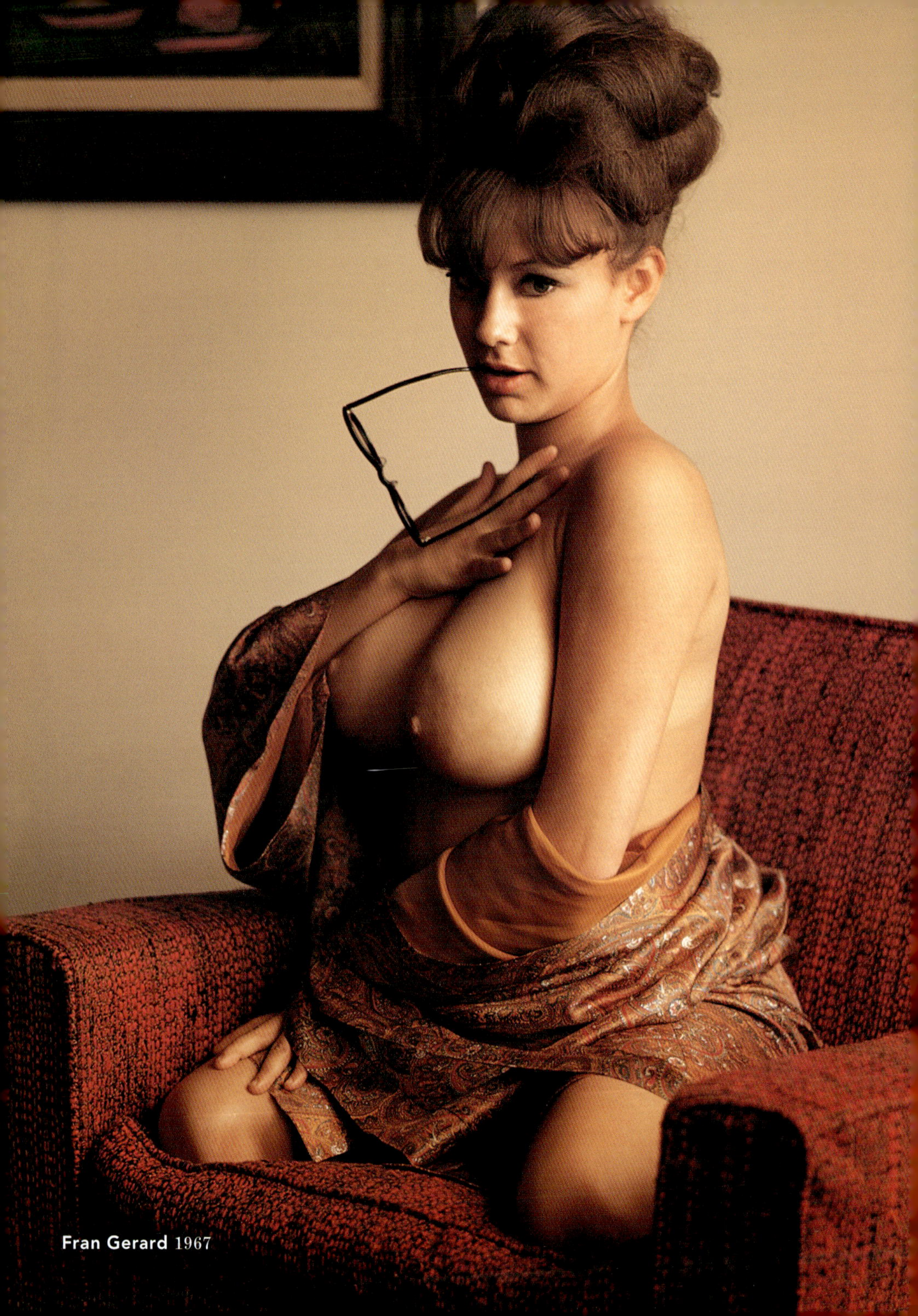
Fran Gerard 1967

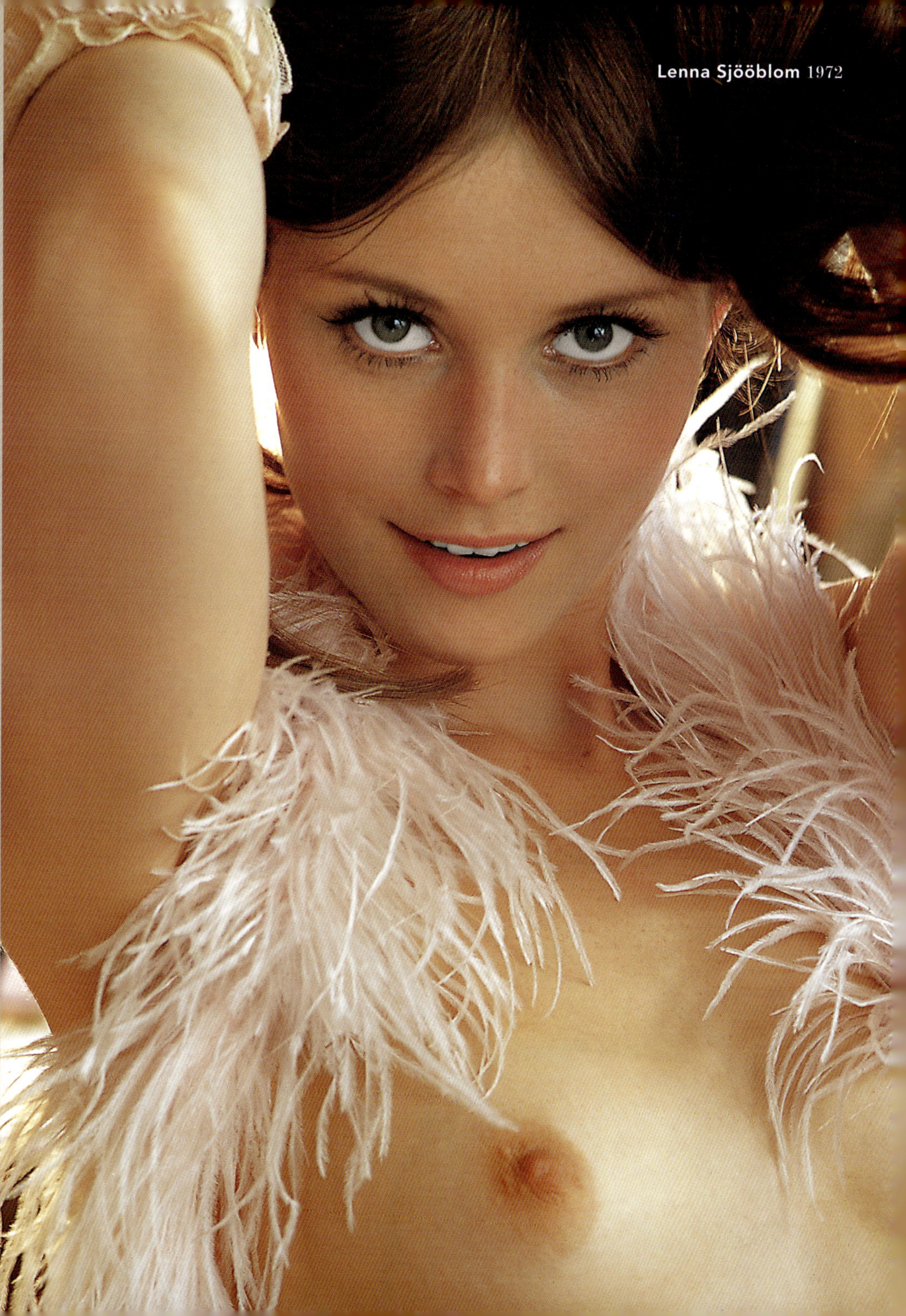

Lenna Sjööblom 1972

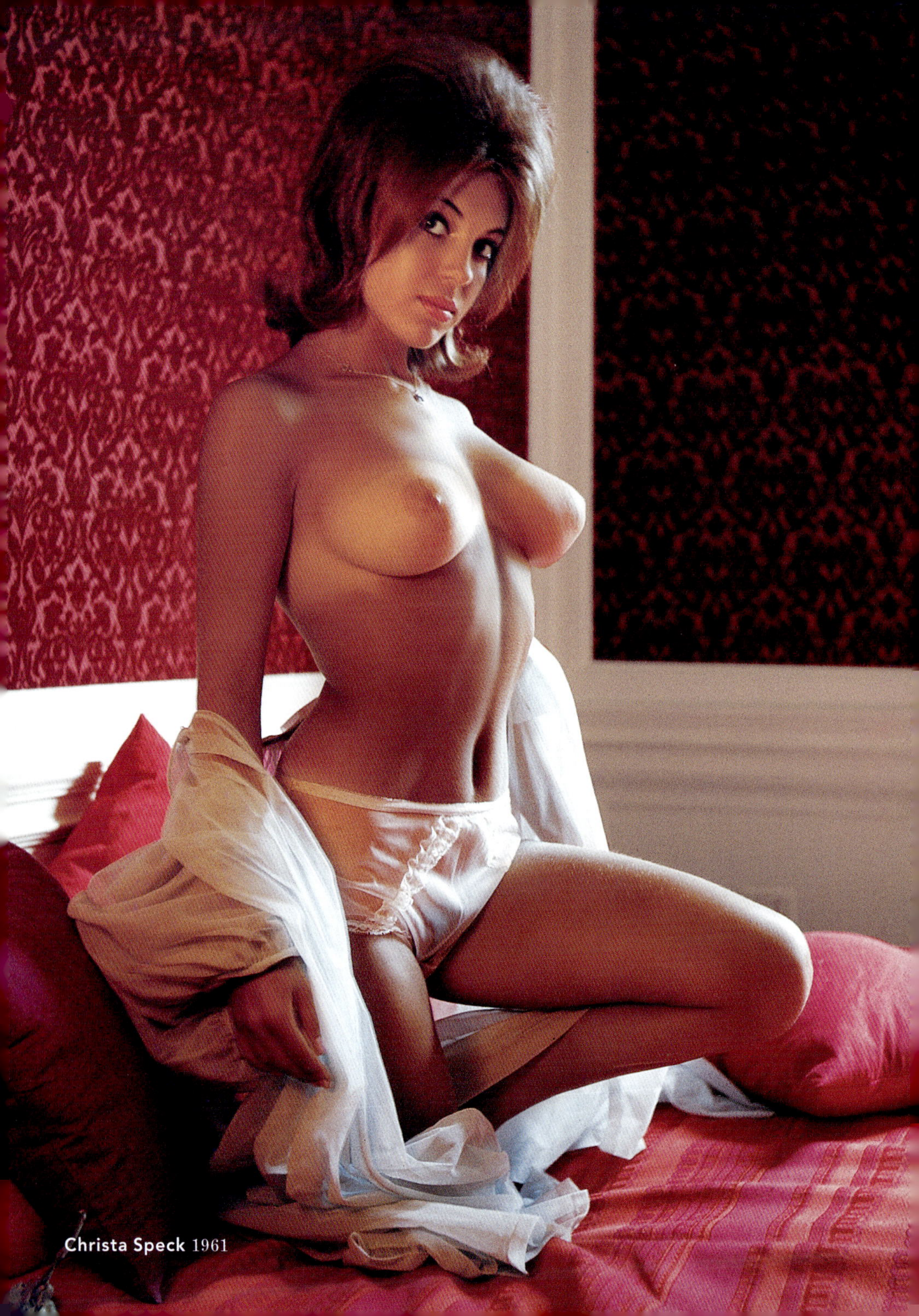

Christa Speck 1961

“Blondes tease . . . brunettes please.”

BUMPER STICKER

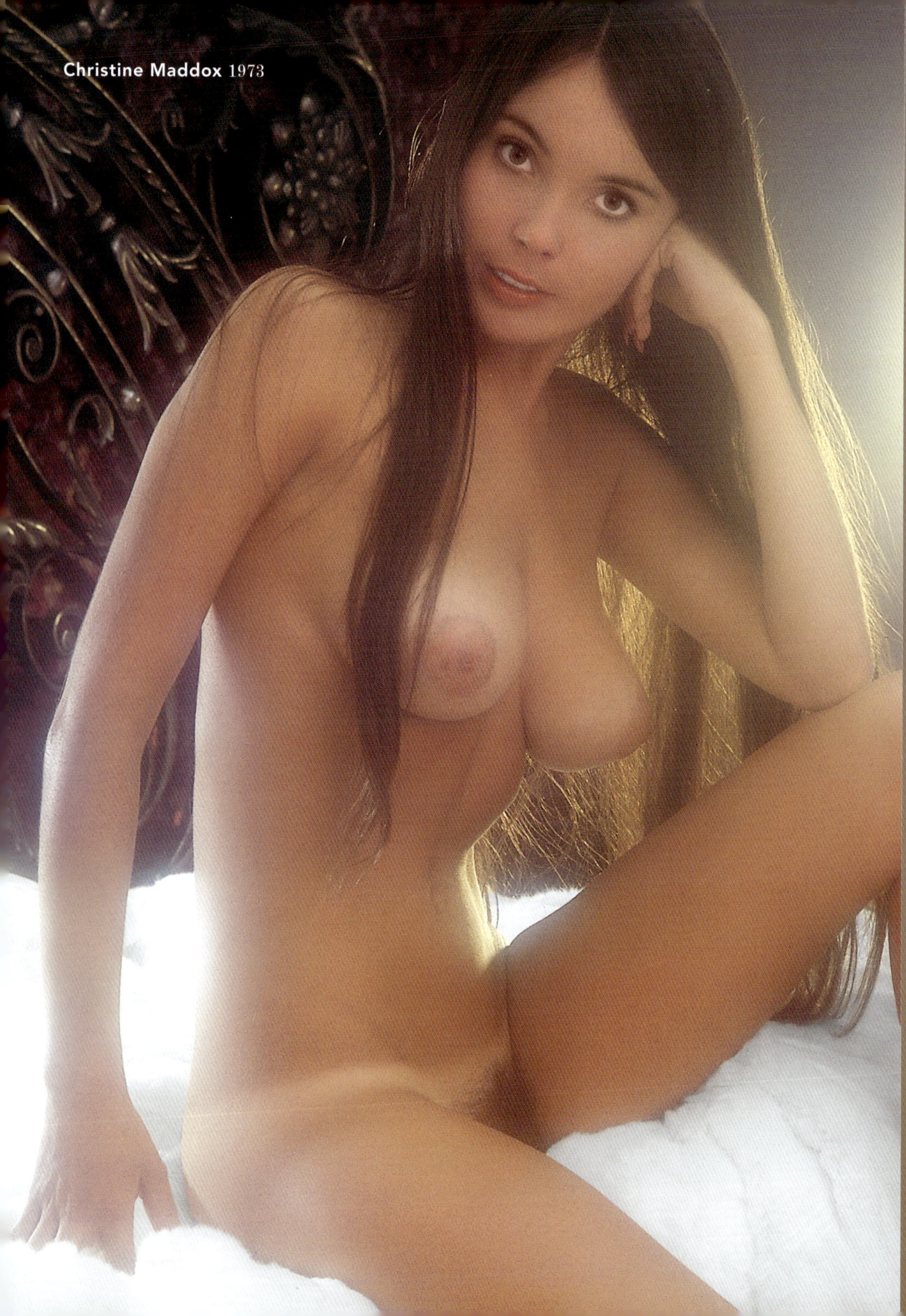

Christine Maddox 1973

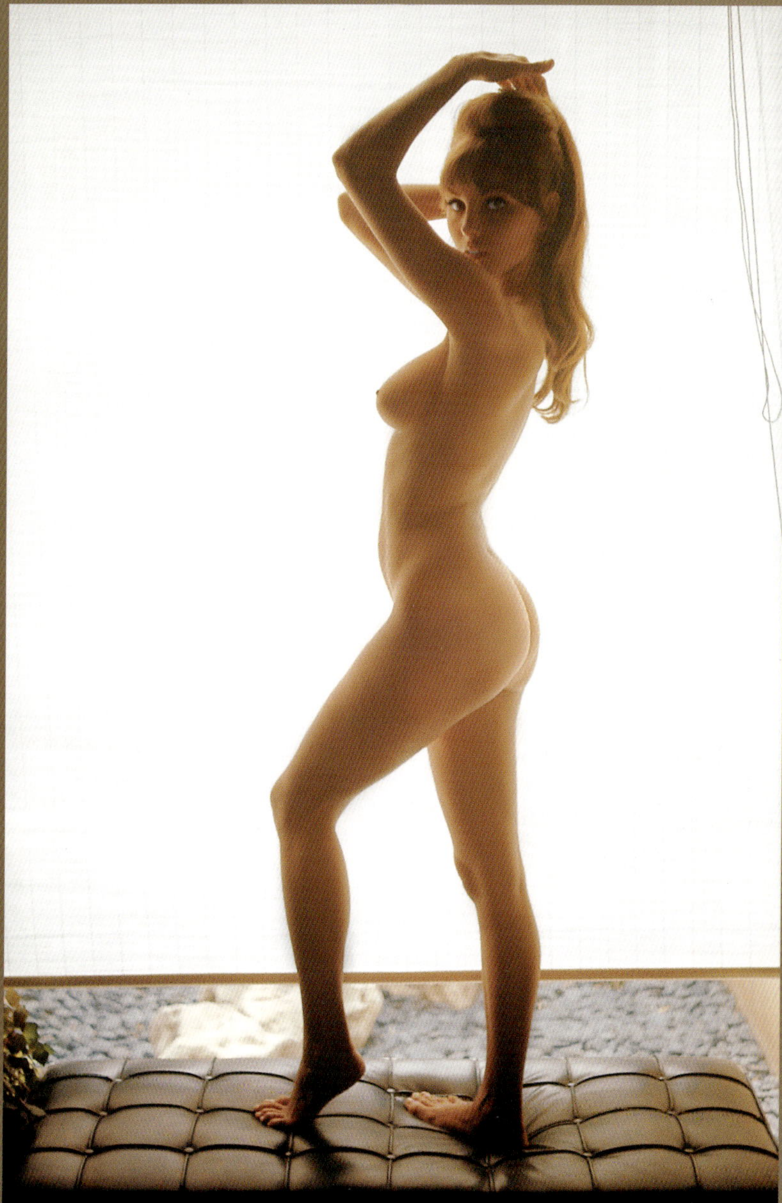

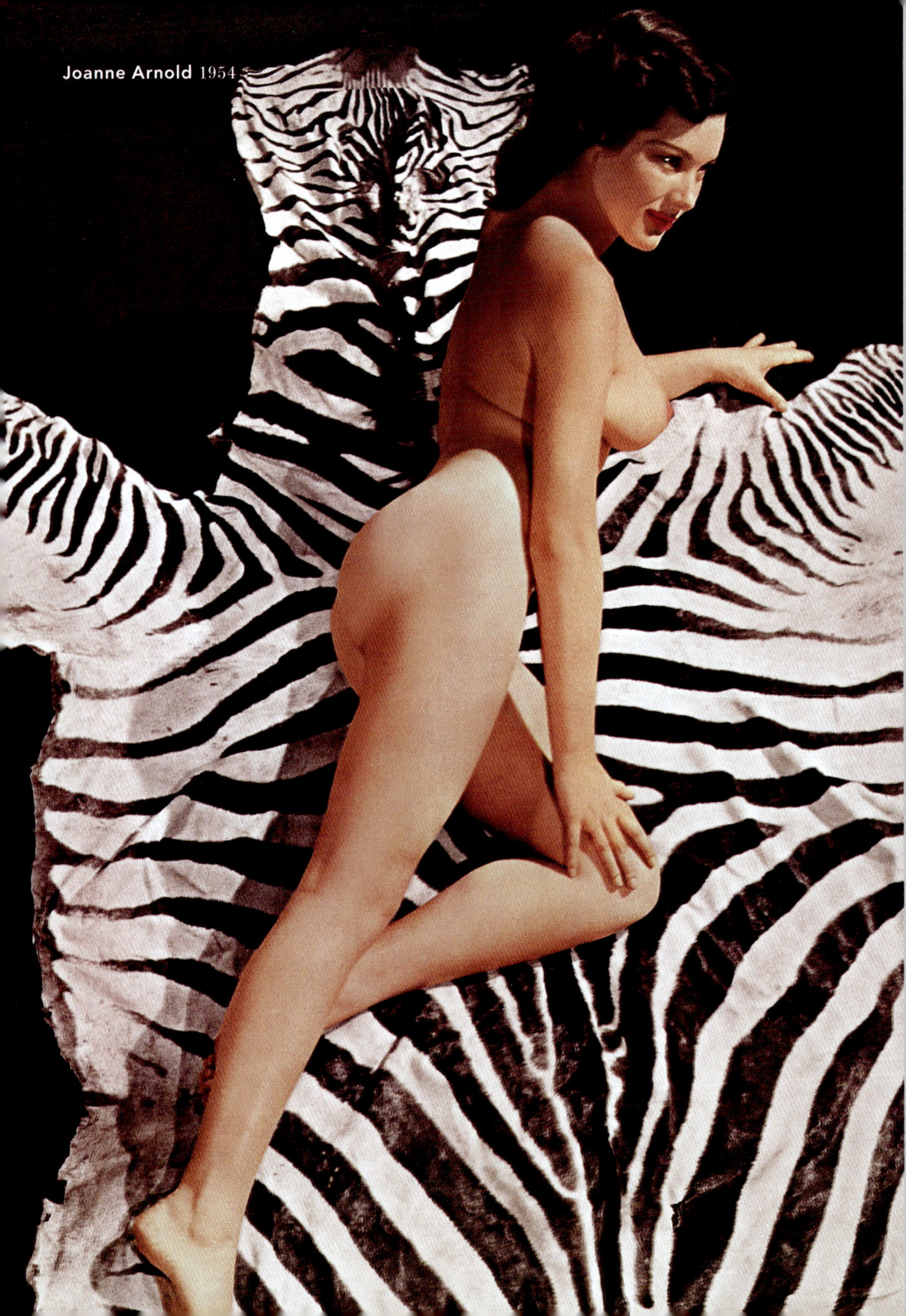

Joanne Arnold 1954

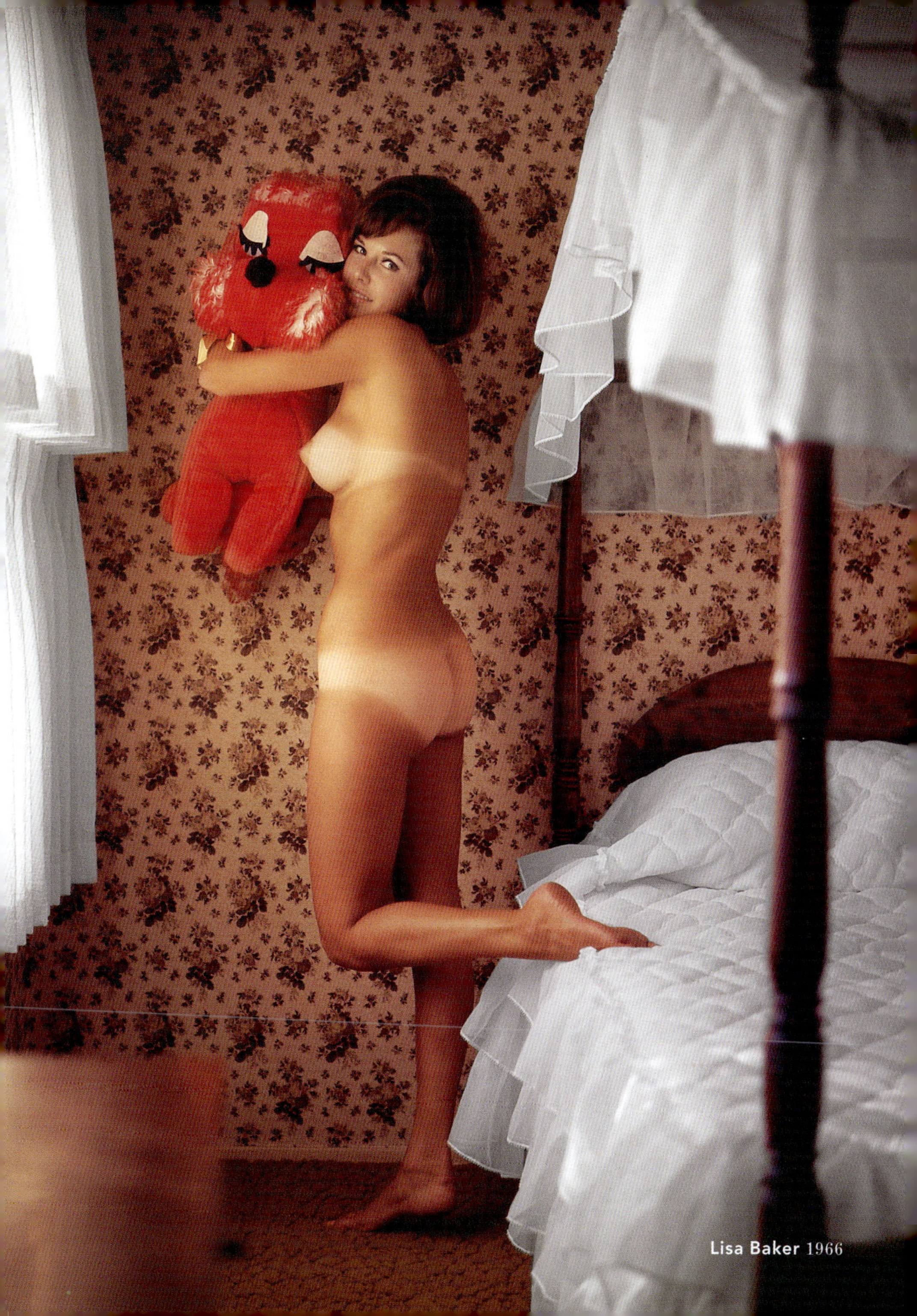

Lisa Baker 1966

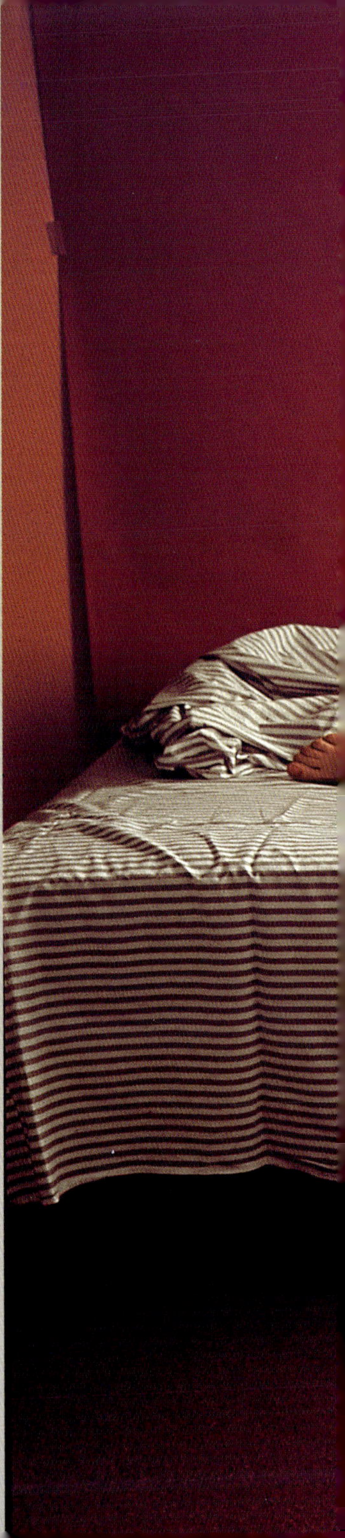

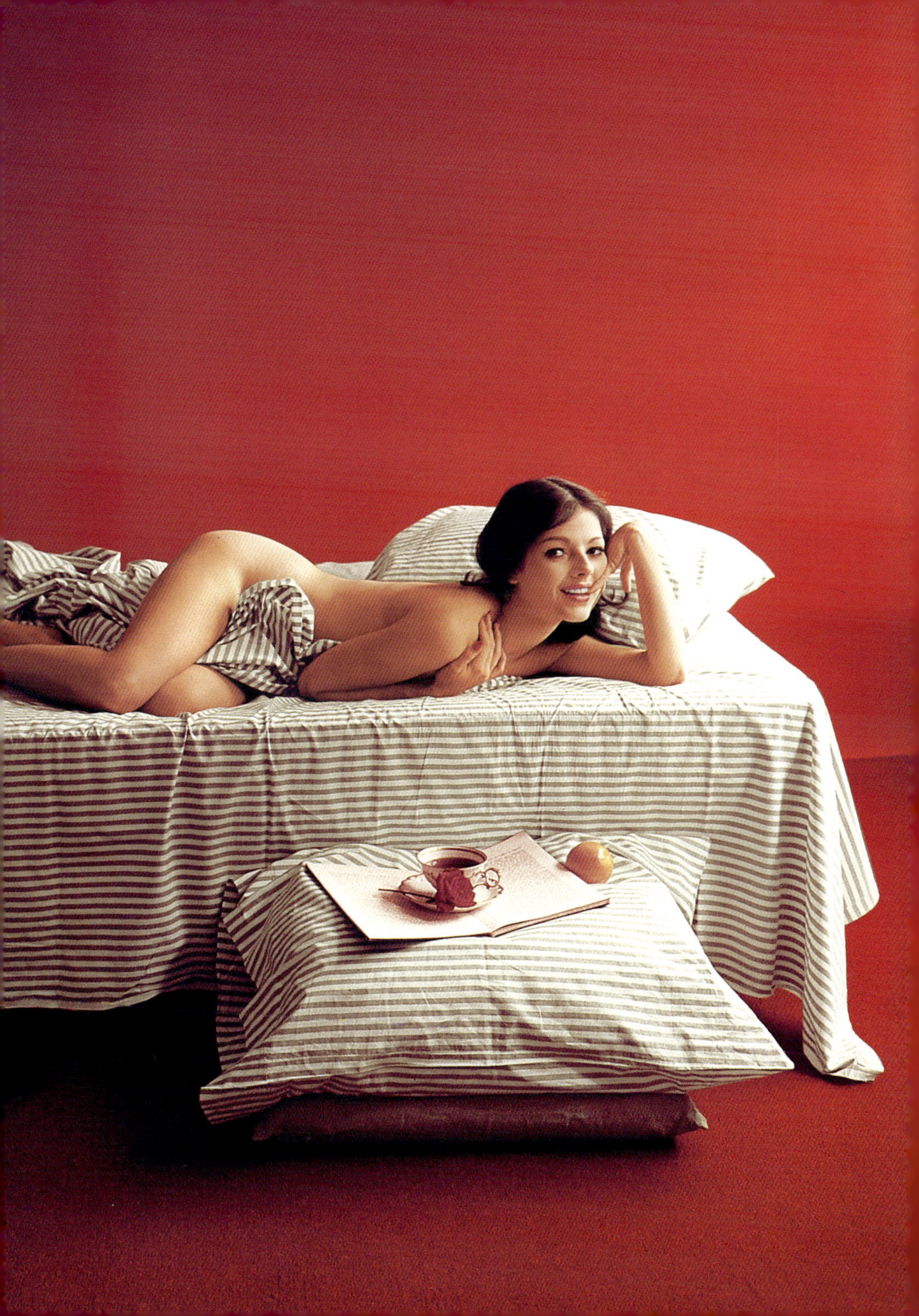

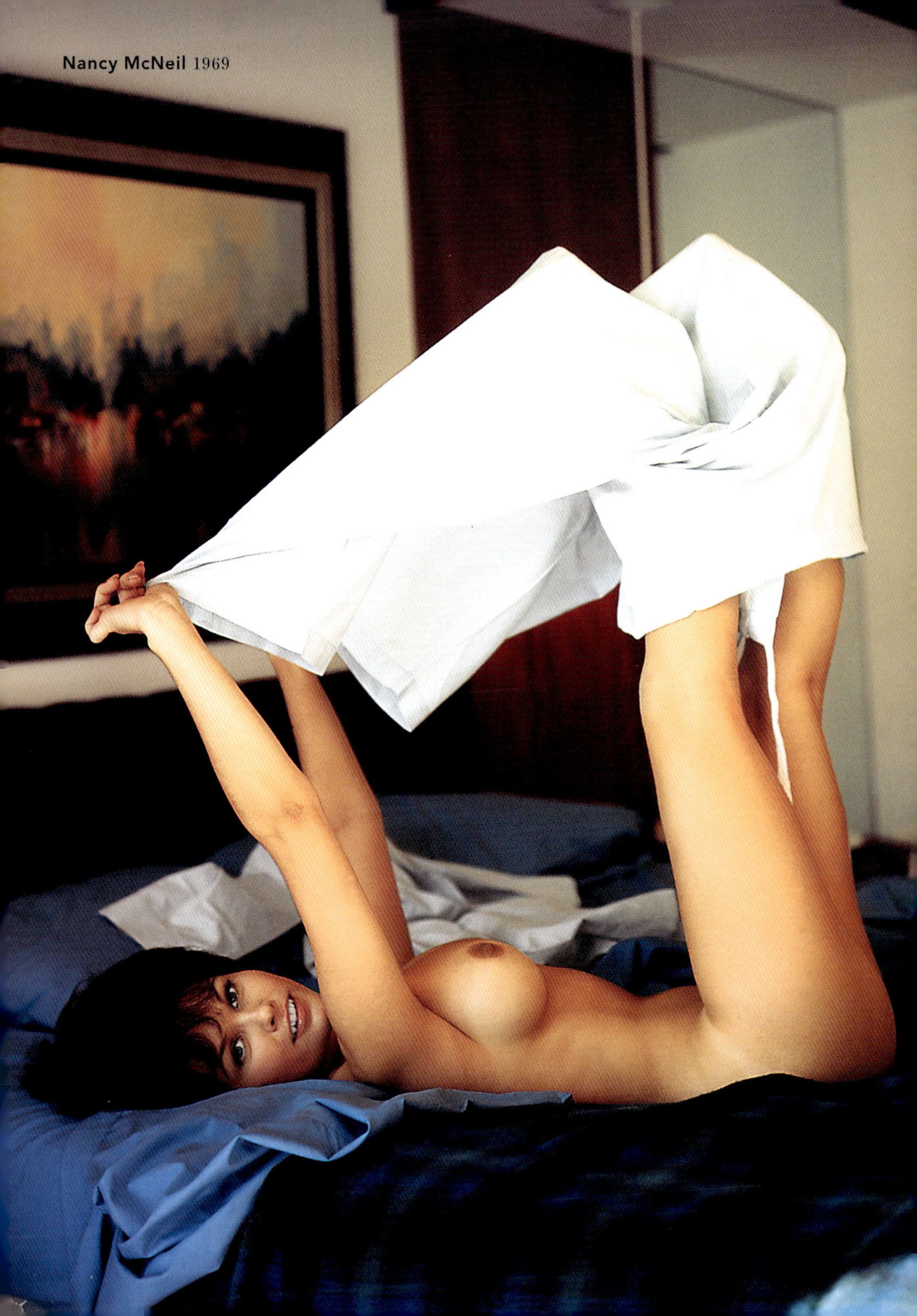

Nancy McNeil 1969

"My line? My most effective one
is to tell a girl she has hair
like a tortured midnight, lips like
a red couch in an ivory palace,
and that I'm lonely and starved for
affection. Then, I generally
burst into tears. It seldom works."

FROM *GENTLEMEN PREFER BLONDES*

Sandra Edwards 1957

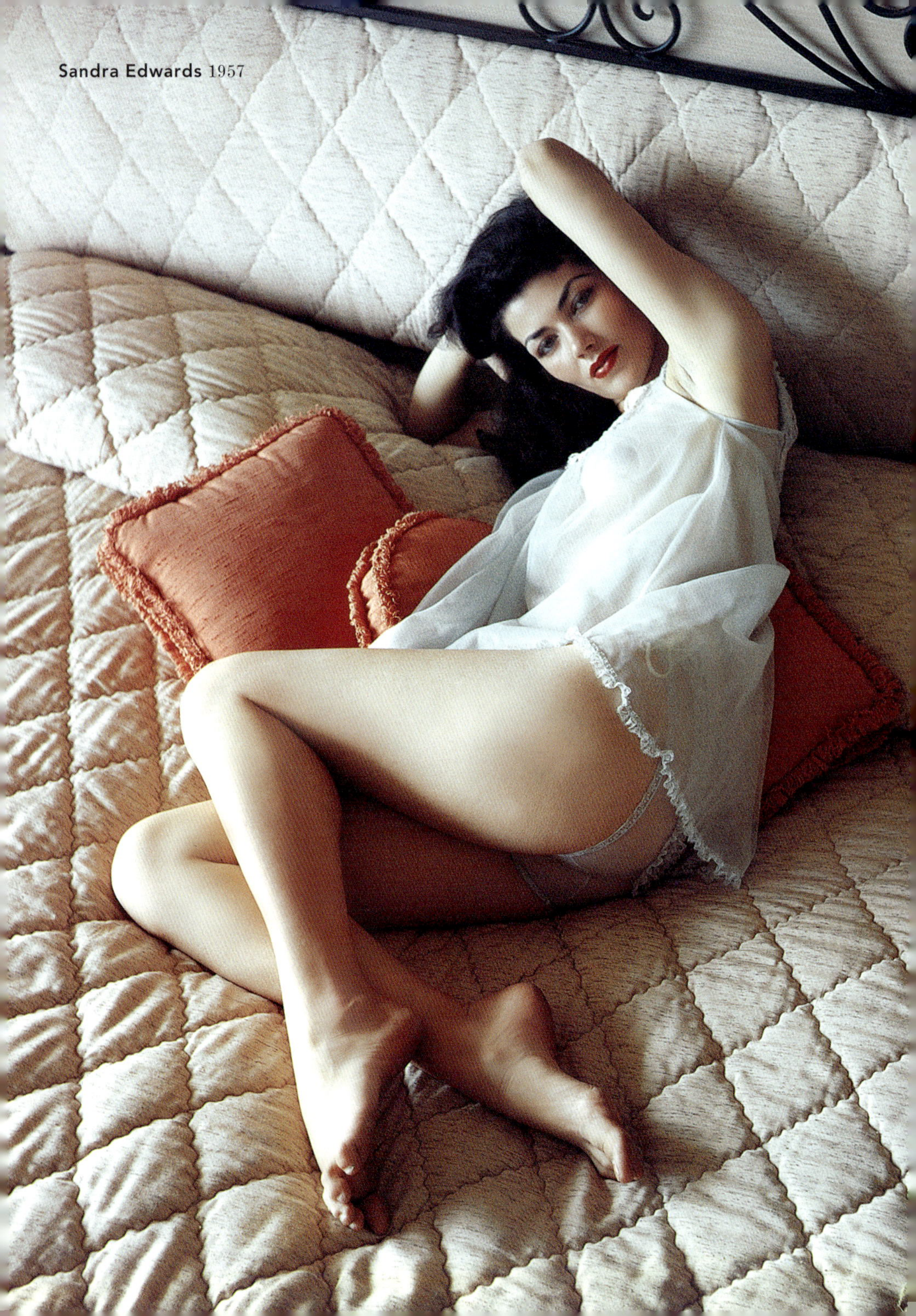

Jean Jani 1957

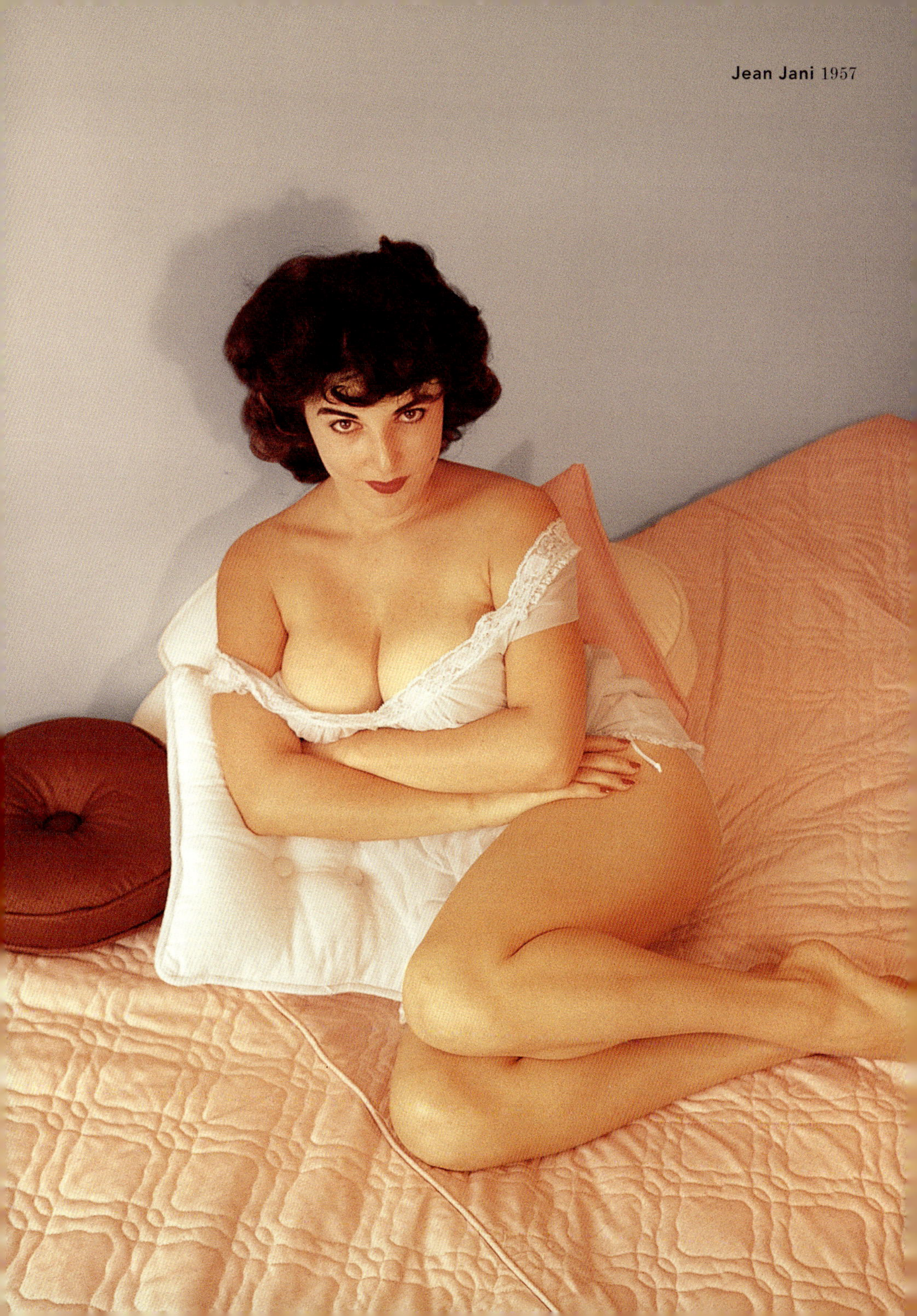

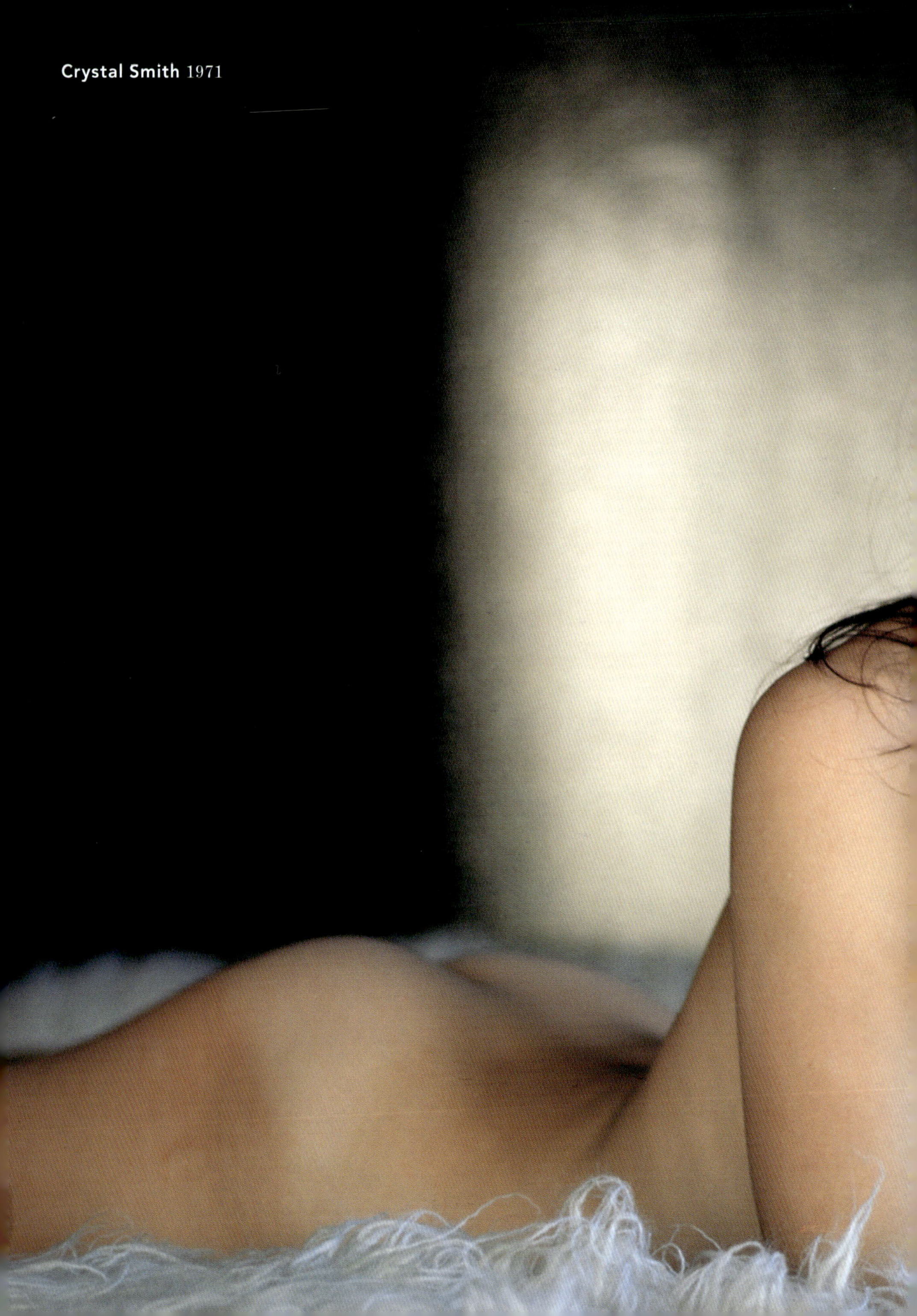

Crystal Smith 1971

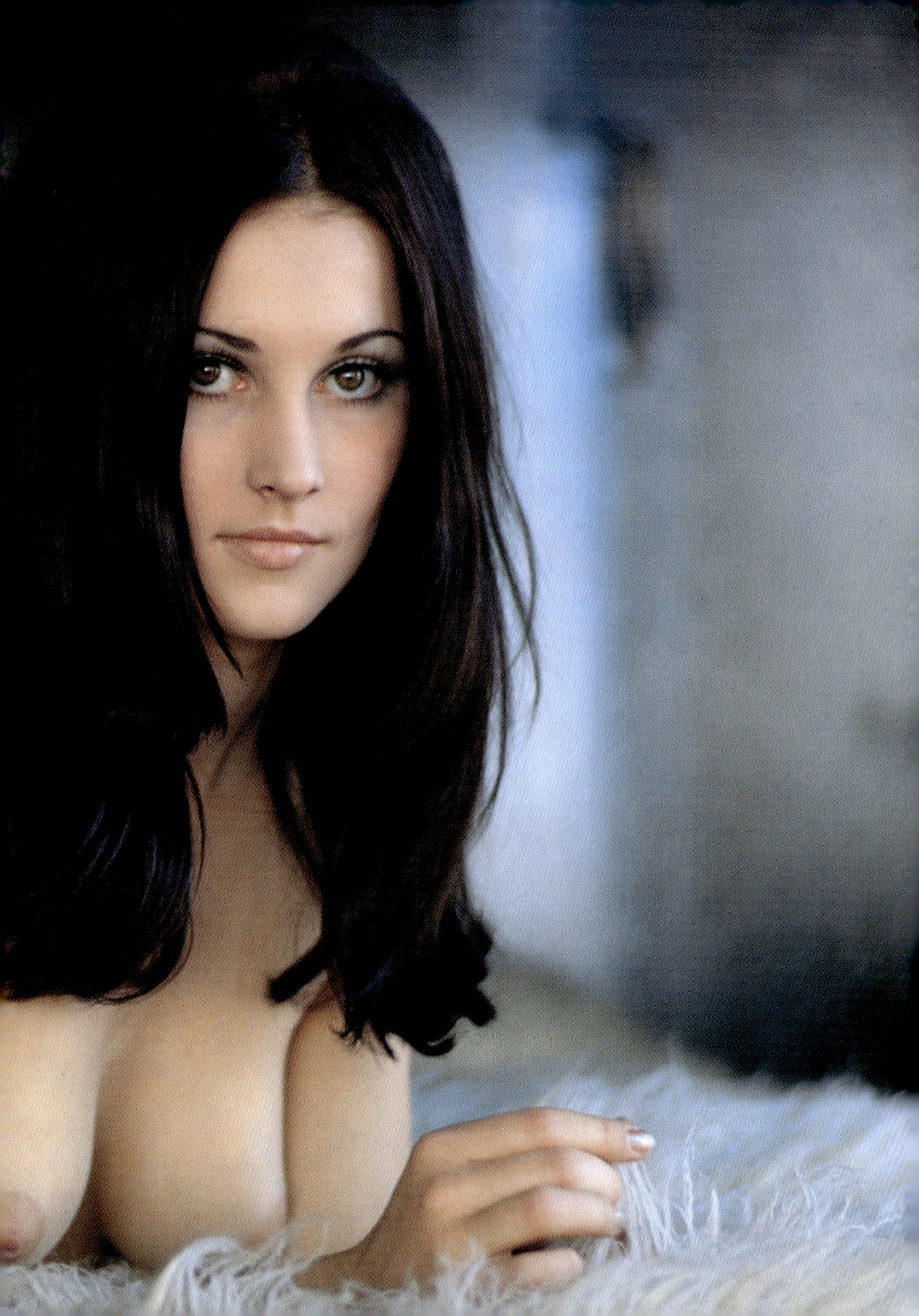

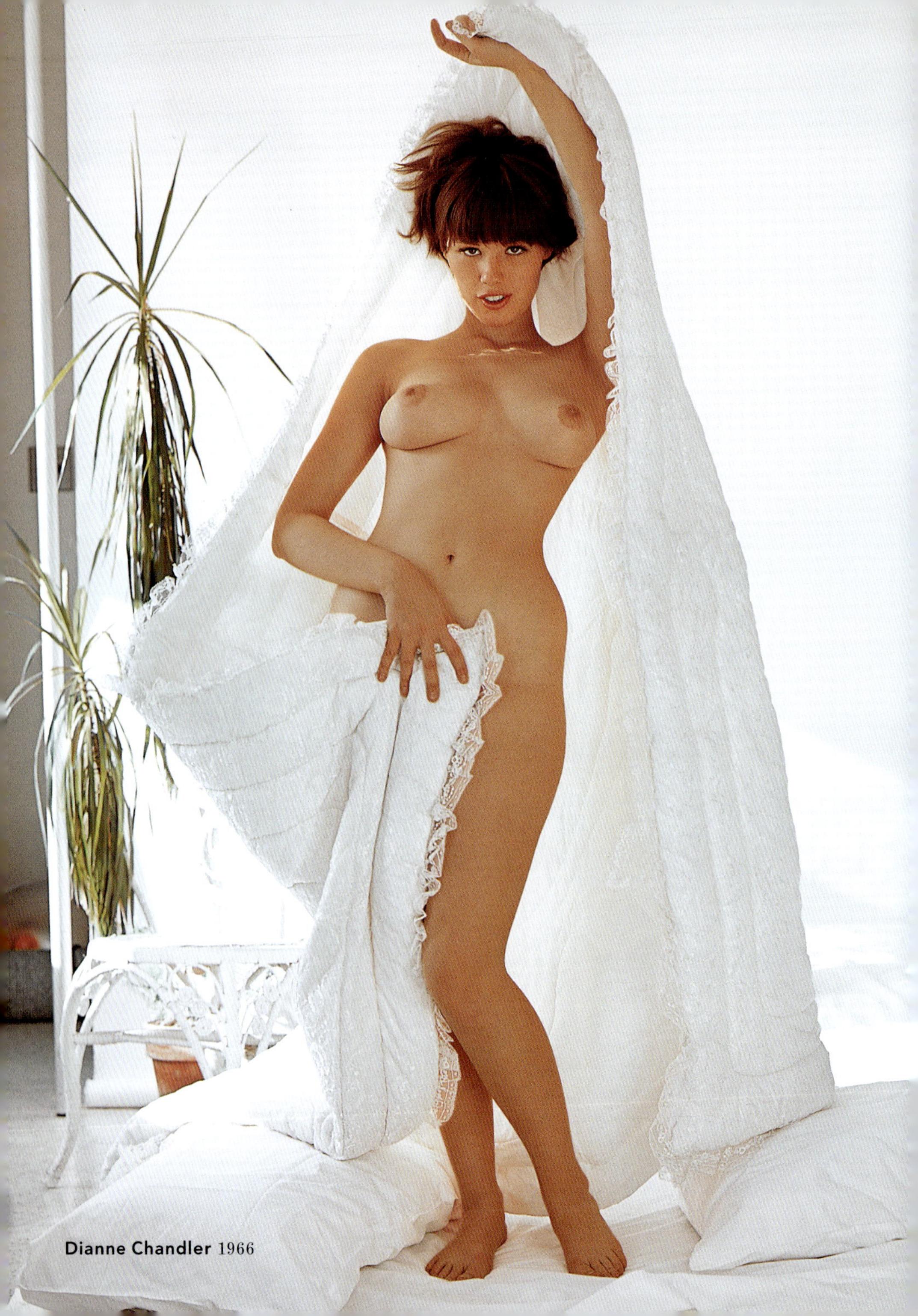

Dianne Chandler 1966

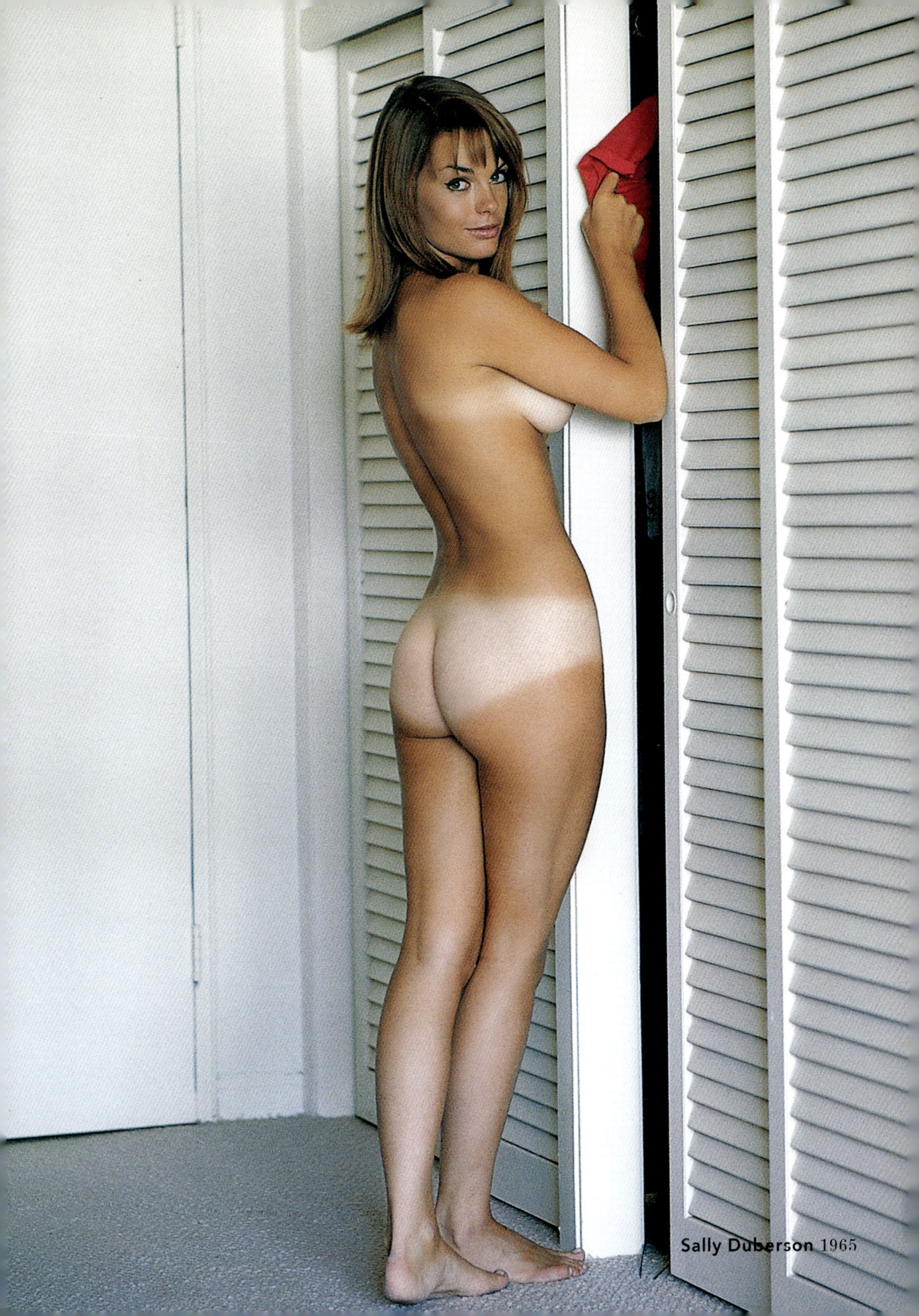

Sally Duberson 1965

“My fans want me with my hair.”

SARAH BRIGHTMAN (A BRUNETTE)

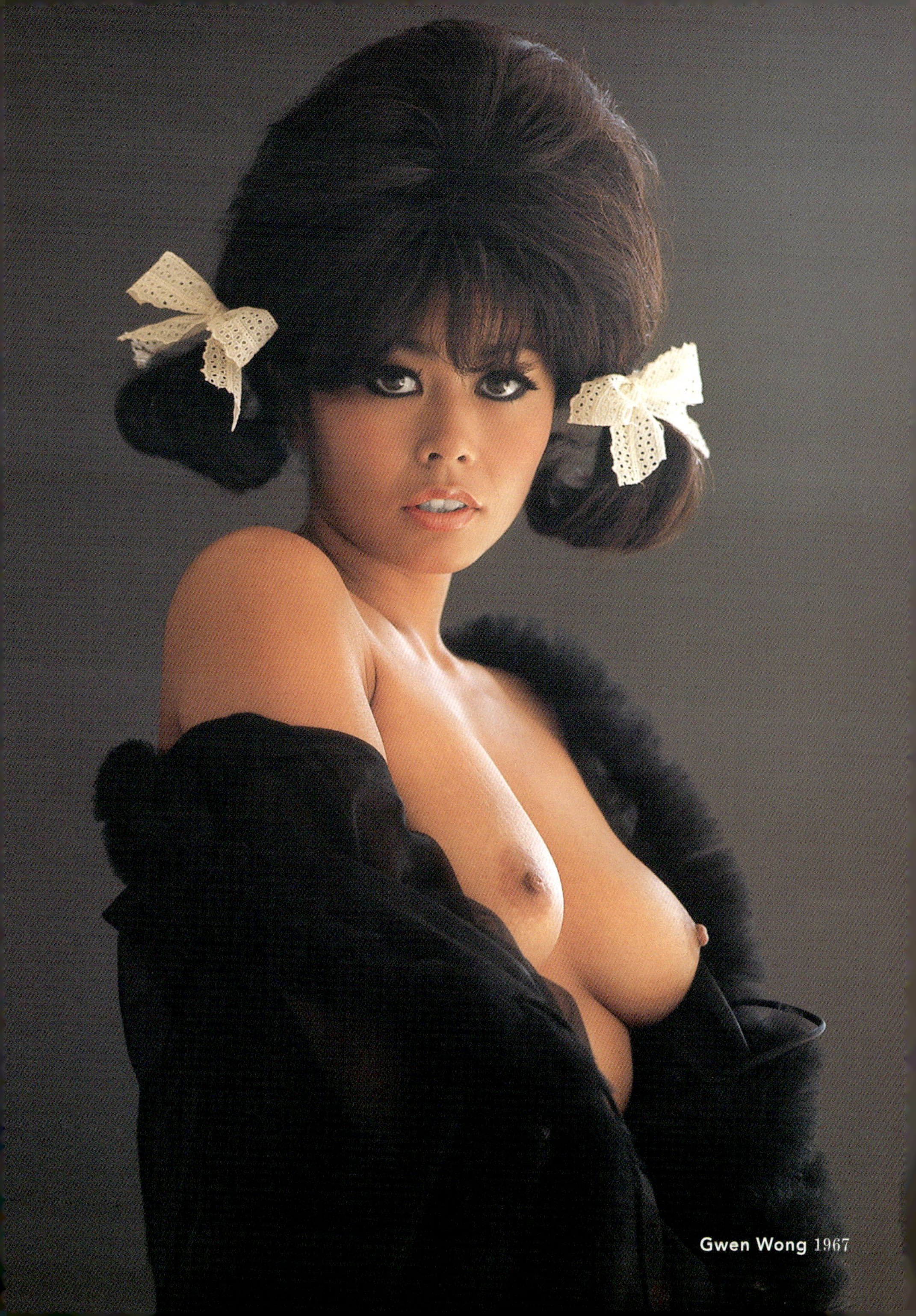

Gwen Wong 1967

Kai Brendlinger 1964

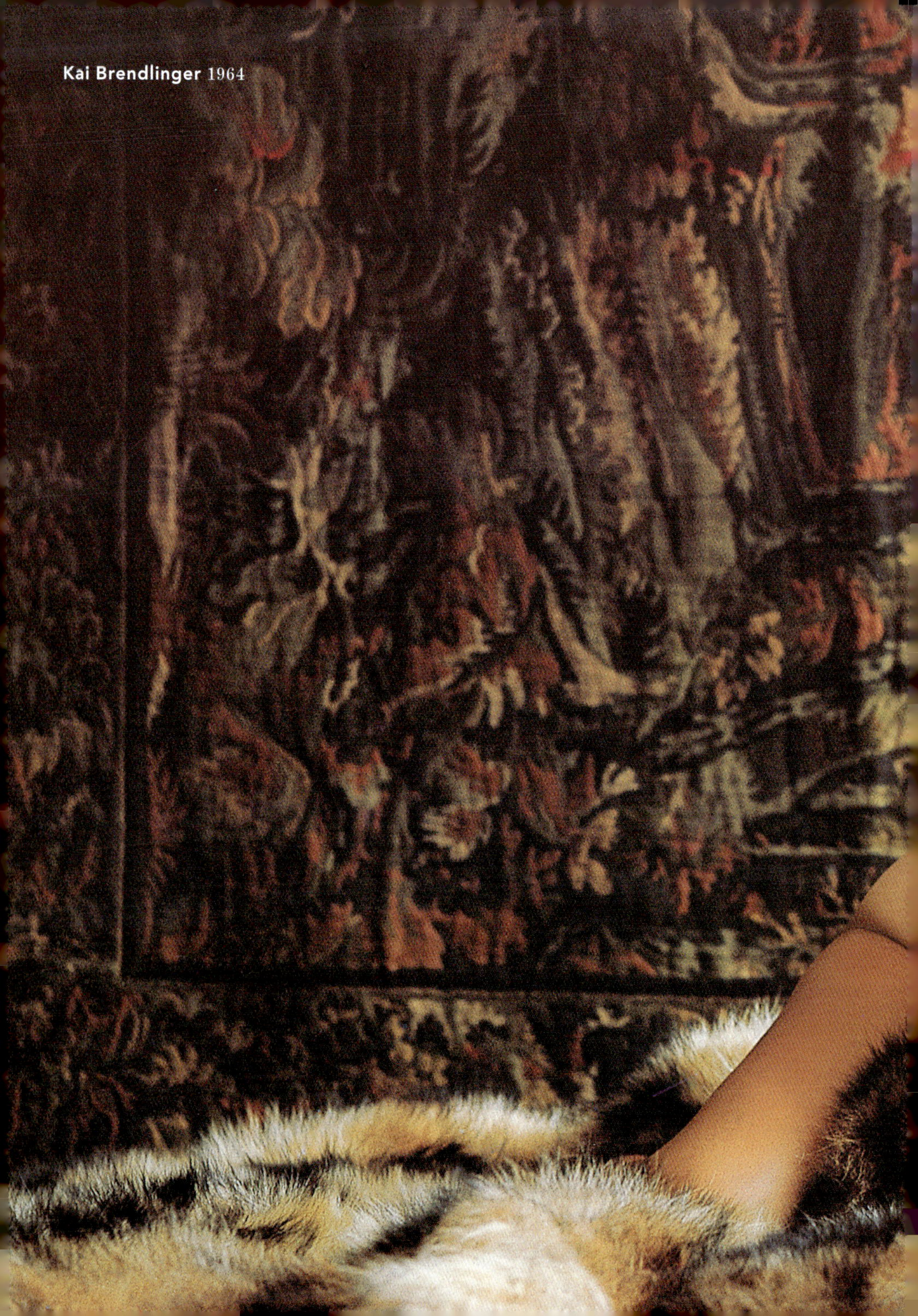

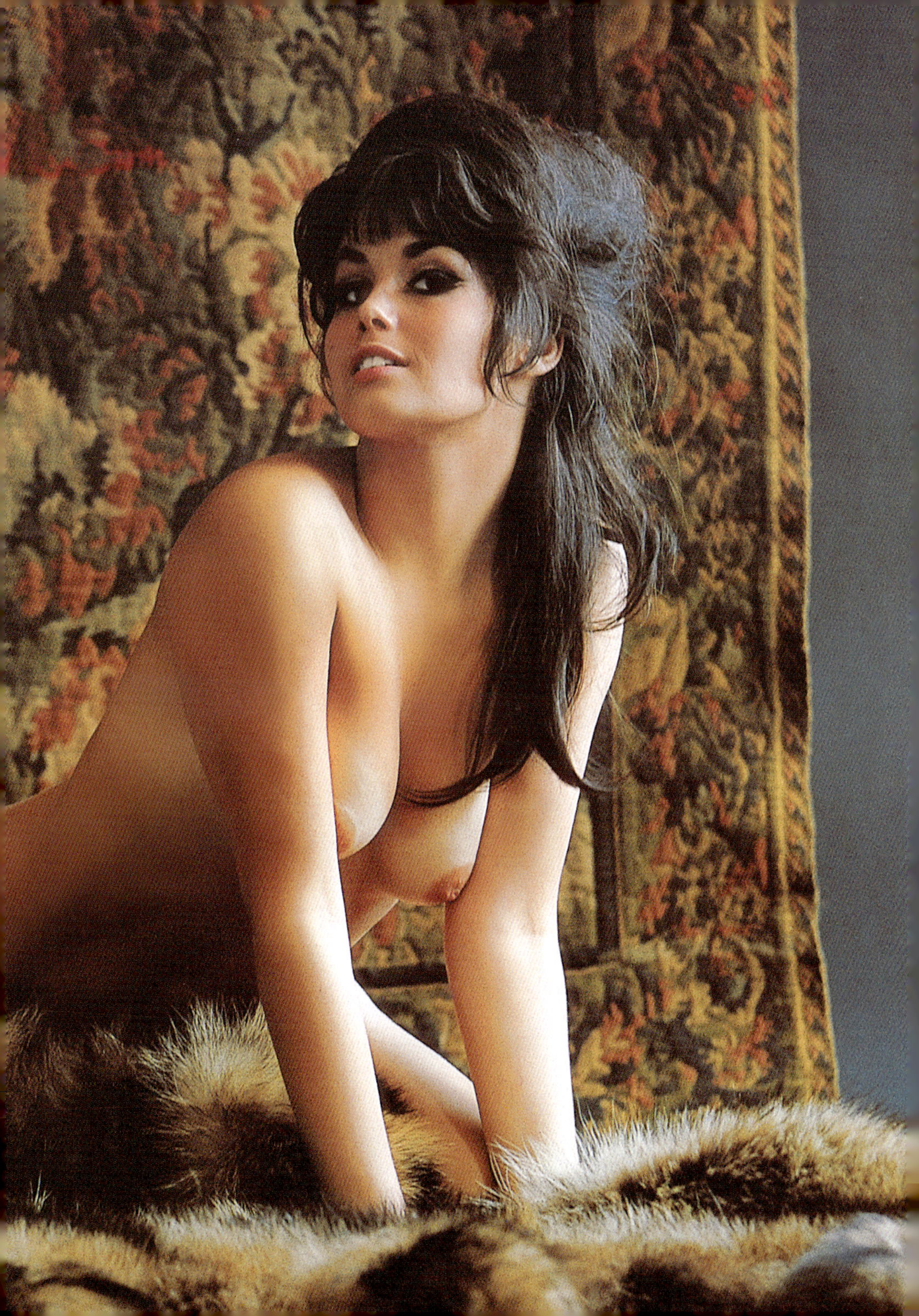

CREDITS BY PHOTOGRAPHER

Adams, Hal *51, 56–57*
Blackwell, Carlyle *67*
Bronstein, Don *101*
Casilli, Mario *43, 45, 52, 53, 60, 66, 78, 80–81, 84–85, 86, 87, 96–97, 98, 99, 104, 106, 123*
Chan, David *17, 26, 39, 62, 71, 72–73*
Eck, Frank *48*
Figge, Bill *111*
Figge, Bill & Mel *23, 24–25, 31, 55*
Figge/DeLong *14–15, 40, 44, 68–69, 70, 100, 114*
Gowland, Peter *110, 116, 117*
Gunther, Curt *34–35, 109*
Hooker, Dwight *38, 49, 77, 83, 92–93, 105, 118–119*
John Baumgarth Co. *2*
Melford, H. *18–19*
O'Rourke, J. Barry *46–47*
Otto, Glenn *12–13*
Posar, Pompeo *20, 22, 41, 58, 59, 65, 79, 90, 94, 103, 108, 121, 124–125*
Schiller, Lawrence *64*
Smith, Paul *29, 30, 74–75*
Sutton, David *88*
Urba, Alexas *27, 120*
Vogel, Ron *5, 17, 36, 42, 91*
White, Jerry *112–113*
Wilson, R. *63*
Yeager, Bunny *16, 32*

CREDITS BY PAGE

2 John Baumgarth Co.
5 Ron Vogel
12–13 Glenn Otto
14–15 Figge/DeLong
16 Bunny Yeager
17 David Chan
17 Ron Vogel
18–19 H. Melford
20 Pompeo Posar
22 Pompeo Posar
23 Bill & Mel Figge
24–25 Bill & Mel Figge
26 David Chan
27 Alexas Urba
29 Paul Smith
30 Paul Smith
31 Bill & Mel Figge
32 Bunny Yeager
34–35 Curt Gunther
36 Ron Vogel
38 Dwight Hooker
39 David Chan
40 Figge/DeLong
41 Pompeo Posar
42 Ron Vogel
43 Mario Casilli
44 Figge/DeLong
45 Mario Casilli
46–47 J. Barry O'Rourke
48 Frank Eck
49 Dwight Hooker
51 Hal Adams
52 Mario Casilli
53 Mario Casilli
55 Bill & Mel Figge
56–57 Hal Adams
58 Pompeo Posar
59 Pompeo Posar
60 Mario Casilli
62 David Chan
63 R. Wilson
64 Lawrence Schiller
65 Pompeo Posar
66 Mario Casilli
67 Carlyle Blackwell
68–69 Figge/DeLong
70 Figge/DeLong
71 David Chan
72–73 David Chan
74–75 Paul Smith
77 Dwight Hooker
78 Mario Casilli
79 Pompeo Posar
80–81 Mario Casilli
83 Dwight Hooker
84–85 Mario Casilli
86 Mario Casilli
87 Mario Casilli
88 David Sutton
90 Pompeo Posar
91 Ron Vogel
92–93 Dwight Hooker
94 Pompeo Posar
96–97 Mario Casilli
98 Mario Casilli
99 Mario Casilli
100 Figge/DeLong
101 Don Bronstein
103 Pompeo Posar
104 Mario Casilli
105 Dwight Hooker
106 Mario Casilli
108 Pompeo Posar
109 Curt Gunther
110 Peter Gowland
111 Bill Figge
112–113 Jerry White
114 Figge/DeLong
116 Peter Gowland
117 Peter Gowland
118–119 Dwight Hooker
120 Alexas Urba
121 Pompeo Posar
123 Mario Casilli
124–125 Pompeo Posar

Many thanks and warm acknowledgments to everyone at *Playboy*—without their expertise and commitment this project would have been impossible: Gary Cole, Leopold Froehlich, Hugh Hefner, Bonnie Jean Kenny, Malina Lee, Bradley Lincoln, James R. Petersen, Jessica Riddle, Howard Shapiro, Tom Staebler, and Marcia Terrones.